A Carpenter's Advice on Buying a Home

Brief ▪ Concise ▪ Practical
How to Choose Quality

Written and Illustrated by
Greg Evans

Canary ConnecT™

Published by
Canary Connect Publications
A Division of SOBOLE, Inc.
Coralville, IA

DISCLAIMER

This publication is designed to provide competent and reliable information regarding the subject matter covered. Information contained in this book is the author's opinion based upon years of experience in carpentry and is intended to be useful and educational. While a great deal of care has been taken to provide accurate and current information, some information may be affected by changes in state and federal law (or changes in interpretations of the law) or changes in the home building industry since the manuscript was written. Therefore, the accuracy and completeness of the information contained in this book and the opinions based on it cannot be guaranteed.

The publisher and authors declare that to the best of their knowledge all material in this book is accurate. We shall have neither liability nor responsibility to any person with respect to any loss or damage caused, or alleged to be caused, directly or indirectly, by the information contained in this book.

A Carpenter's Advice on Buying a Home

Cover design by Shannon Heiman Design
Cover illustration by Joyce M. Turley, Dixon Cove Design

ISBN: 0–9643462–2–2
Library of Congress Catalog Number 99–07682

Printed in the United States of America

How to order single or multiple copies: See page 147.

Table of Contents

Table of Figures

Reviews of

A Carpenter's Advice on Buying a Home

This precise and direct book contains a wealth of vital information and should be the first step taken by every future homeowner.

Howard L., MO

Why couldn't I have had a copy of <u>A Carpenter's Advice on Buying A Home</u> when we were trying to buy a home! An easy-to-read, clear, step-by-step guide to points of exploration for any homebuyer. I heartily suggest reading and using this text.

Paul R., IA

<u>A Carpenter's Advice on Buying A Home</u> is a wonderful tool for all homeowners (to evaluate the condition of their home), but even more so for those in the market to buy a home.

It is written in a clear and concise way, concentrating on those aspects of a house which are the most important and are usually only perused by

Continued on next page

an experienced buyer. The illustrations are clear and helpful and the advice is excellent.

I wish this book had been available when I was buying.

Juan G., IA

A Carpenter's Advice on Buying A Home was very impressive. This book was very informative and hard to put down. Every potential homeowner should read it.

Kay F., WI

A Carpenter's Advice on Buying A Home is a great book—and it works! We were struggling with the "buy or build" question and weren't having much luck with either option. This book really helped us feel confident in doing our own home inspection and finding a well-built home we could call our own. We especially liked the "things to look for" information that cued us in to checking things like siding, electrical, framework, etc. We also used a couple of the techniques mentioned—we asked a carpenter friend to check out a promising house and we checked with neighbors in the areas we were considering. This book was just the tool we needed to allow my husband, four children, and myself to move from an over-filled two bedroom apartment into a wonderful home that will give us the "elbow room" we need. Thank you!

Wendy S., IA

Acknowledgements

I'm glad for the opportunity to publicly thank Jesus for this book, not to mention the many other things He has done for me, the volume of which could fill another book.

As far as mortals go, Deb is my favorite. It was her hard work, organization, and persistence that gave this book life. These same qualities bless our family life and a line from a poem* comes to mind when I think of her—"full of hands and full of eyes." She knows no rest. I thank her with a simple poem of my own.

My love for you is conditional,
So please don't rearrange.
I couldn't love you anymore
If you should ever change.
So, curl your hair, buy a dress
And leave the rest alone.
Stay with me and always be
The Debbie that I've known.

*Pablo Neruda's 'Ode to the Liver'

A Carpenter's Advice on Buying a Home

Introduction

Every day across America families commit themselves to perhaps the greatest financial investment of their life without a clue as to the potential disasters lurking in this aspect of the American dream—their new home. A home's amenities, numerous as they may be, are of little value in the absence of a sound mechanical underpinning. This book is designed to give you the accurate, practical, concise information you need for a successful home search.

A report from the Chicago Title and Trust Company shows that nationally in the United States the average home is sold every 11.9 years (averages range from 6.4 years in Arizona to 19.3 years in Maine).

A careful and discriminating homebuyer should view at least a dozen homes. The selection should then be narrowed to three or four to be scrutinized. It is at this point that an "inspection" would be indicated. While inspection services are available to the prospective homebuyer, it is not practical to inspect several properties at $200 or more per inspection. Secondly, time is a factor. To schedule an inspection, wait for completion of the inspection, and then wait for the final evaluation of the home to arrive could take two or more weeks. This time period can be too long for an exceptional house in an active real estate market.

Some homebuyers rely on the advice of the real estate agent regarding the quality of a home. I think it goes without saying that the typical real estate agent's knowledge of the structural integrity and mechanical state of a home is at best limited. His primary concern, in any case, is the sale rather than quality of the home. Additionally, it's not reasonable to expect a real estate agent to wait patiently as you pour over a thick how-to book while touring each home.

Though I may be biased, it is my firm belief that a master carpenter can give you the best general assessment of a home's integrity. If you are shopping for a home, a family member or a friend with a master carpenter's qualifications can be a valuable resource. However, familiarizing yourself with the basics of what to look for in a home's features and a personal knowledge of the tips and traps you may encounter is also valuable. Whether you're looking at a modest rambler or something more elaborate, this manual will assist you in recognizing the features that will distinguish low maintenance and comfortable living from on-going repair and headache situations.

Each chapter focuses on one aspect of the home with **critical** defects highlighted in **bold** and *serious* defects in *italic* type. I believe that the **critical** defects listed represent the most common major shortcomings in troublesome homes. A checklist of these two types of defects—**critical** and *serious* (or lesser)—that may be used when viewing a home is provided on pages 138–139 with extra copies at the end of this book, beginning on page 149. The information provided, used with the checklist, will allow the homebuyer to confidently inspect the basic features of a prospective home and avoid the confusion of looking at relatively inconsequential details. My general advice is to pass over a home that has any **critical** defects as well as a home with two or more *serious* defects. This rule, of course, may be modified if the home has other outstanding features that compensate for the defect(s).

Remember, when buying a home your best advantage lies in acquiring the basic knowledge that will help you find the home of your dreams. Best wishes for success as you begin your home buying adventure.

The Master Carpenter's Qualifications

In addition to the formal textbook curriculum which includes study in the areas of draftsmanship, engineering, design, and construction of structures, Master Carpenters spend a tremendous amount of time studying wood, hands on. As with any field of study, I believe it is this 'hands on' exposure that is so vital and which qualifies the carpenter to state the rather startling findings included in Chapter 1.

In my own experience, I have sorted through literally 10's of thousands of boards selecting oak, cherry, black walnut, white pine, southern yellow pine, Douglas fir, redwood, cedar; quarter-sawn or flat-sawn; moisture content, type of curing or kiln-drying; origin of the wood; and so on. I have cut, sawed, planed, shaped, coped, and molded virtually every wood common to the Midwest and beyond. I have cut and fit every type of plywood, oriented strand board, laminate, and solid board you can name. I machine them, fill my eyes with the dust, and know their individual smells, hardness, and other characteristics. Lumberyards are my second home. Much of my time is spent there and I am on a first name basis with all their personnel. I know their inventories better than most of the employees.

In addition, since remodeling jobs make up a good deal of my business, I do a lot of demolition (disassembling) of walls, floors, and ceilings which provides information on how well the material has held up. The difficulty or ease of disassembly is a telltale sign as to quality.

To summarize, with all the hands-on experience involved, I don't know who could better judge the quality (or lack thereof) of home building materials and their application than a Master Carpenter—the professional most familiar with them.

Over time, the Master Carpenter also has the opportunity to witness the changes occurring in the building industry—for better and for worse. My personal experiences have led me to develop definite opinions on the quality of current home-building materials (discussed in Chapter 1) and to a desire to educate others regarding the home features to seek and to avoid. Some people simply cannot fathom what is actually happening in the area of home construction today. I might be skeptical myself, were I not in the trade. The need for providing this information is illustrated in the following example.

A customer from here in Iowa City, an intelligent man and school teacher whose wife is an associate professor at the University of Iowa, contacted me when his daughter and her husband were looking for a house to buy. He hired me to do an inspection on one they really liked. He knew me to be a carpenter dissatisfied with current building trends and someone who appreciated the quality in older homes. I inspected the home and found it was a nice, solid home built, I believe, in the 1960's. It passed my inspection with good grades. Unfortunately, the home seller sold it by bids and their bid fell short of the mark.

This same customer called me back a few weeks later with another proposition. Would I oversee construction of a new home for his daughter and son-in-law? I declined, reiterating my feelings on the situation of the poor quality of building materials in use today and that I would not feel comfortable being responsible for a new home. This man just could not accept the reality of the poor quality of home building materials across the nation. (However, quality is much better in some regions, such as the Northwest.) The notion to him was incredible and he told me so. He asked, "Do you have any idea how serious and widespread an indictment you're making?"

I do realize how hard the situation is to accept. But that only accentuates the need for the information to be made available. This is one of the reasons I wrote this book.

Chapter 1

New Homes—An Exposé

I don't think you need to be an ecologist to recognize the environmental dangers in our world today and the resulting effects of these factors. In much of the United States, exorbitant water bill rates reflect the cost of building new water treatment facilities to continue the challenge of removing farm chemicals, industrial waste, and other pollutants from our once pristine wells and rivers. In a report that was widely perceived to be conservative (released in the mid 1990's), the Federal Environmental Protection Agency declared over half of our nation's rivers and streams unfit for fishing and swimming.

The number of Americans with allergies has doubled in the last 20 years. Allergies often indicate a weakened immune system and medical research indicates that the immune system may be compromised by repeated insults and challenges made to it. The Centers for Disease Control estimates that up to six million Americans suffer from a weakened immune system. Americans show 100 substances in their blood that were not there 50 years ago. Sperm count in U.S. males is down by 50% since World War II. In the United States, a significant increase in the incidence of cancer is being seen. In Iowa, for instance, there has been a 41% increase in new cancers in the last two decades, and a 28% rise in prostate cancer between the years 1990 and 1991 alone. Even allowing for improved diagnostic methods, these figures are noteworthy. Genetic engineers are currently striving to alter our biological makeup, so we may better fend off man-made carcinogens.

What does this have to do with home buying? Cheap, poor quality materials formerly used only in mobile homes and generally regarded by many carpenters and contractors as junk (until the wood shortage became an issue) are now the materials of choice in new homes in the United States and abroad. If we hope to increase an awareness of the threats to our health, well being, and survival, we need to be aware that newer home construction can include these low-quality materials and that they are full of noxious chemicals.

A few years ago, on a remodeling job, a full piece of paneling came into contact with my bare chest as I carried it across the room. My chest was moist with perspiration and when the paneling touched it I thought I had been branded. My chest felt as if it were on fire. When I pushed the paneling away, I saw a bright red rash (not an abrasion). This reaction occurred in just seconds. Many of the biological threats in our environment today are invisible and with a little encouragement from the business community, we sometimes convince ourselves that they have been overstated. I had read of the dangers of formaldehyde, but this personal experience was very convincing.

The paneling in question was new, expensive, top-of-the-line. The back was stamped with a warning that during installation windows should be open and there should be cross ventilation because of fumes from the formaldehyde-resin glue that bonds the plywood layers together. (Formaldehyde-resin glue came into wide use in the late 1970's.) The manufacturer's warning to open windows during installation is often impractical since many interior remodel jobs are carried out during the winter months. Furthermore, paneling is primarily a basement wall finish where windows are rare.

In newer construction, this same formaldehyde-resin glue is also present in the plywood, particleboard, and oriented strand board (also known as OSB, Ox-board, or waferboard). While particle board is not widely used in exterior applications, OSB is gaining in use as a sheathing material largely due to the fact that its cost is roughly half that of plywood. Sheathing is the term used for the 4x8 foot sheets (commonly plywood or OSB) that are applied to a house's walls and roof prior to siding and shingle application.

Let's look at oriented strand board (OSB), a glue bonded, wood chip composite board that came into widespread use in the late 1980's. OSB is notorious for its nearly intolerable fumes. Carpenters suffer from irritation of the throat, watery eyes, and headaches when working with OSB. Some carpenters are simply unable to work with it. In addition, OSB deteriorates, swells, and falls apart when it is in contact with excessive moisture. The emergence of the use of plastic house wraps and OSB sheathing in home construction occurred (not coincidentally) simultaneously in the late 1980's. I believe plastic house wraps were developed to protect the OSB against moisture even though the manufacturers would probably not acknowledge this product's weakness.

Now consider this: after a new home has been covered with a plastic house wrap such as Tyvek (applied underneath the siding to draft-proof the home and protect against moisture) and shingles, these formaldehyde fumes cannot escape to the outside and dissipate. Even if ventilation is possible during construction, what protects the homeowner from the formaldehyde fumes once the carpenters have left?

Plywood sheathing was already somewhat of a compromise, as compared to the solid board construction of a few decades ago. Now a further compromise has occurred with the use of OSB and particleboard as wall, floor, and roof sheathing in homes today. Kitchen cabinets may also be constructed of these materials.

Incredible as it may seem, I have replaced entire roofs that are less than 10 years old because of weak

OSB sheathing. This material is not nearly as strong as plywood and when ½" OSB spans rafters on 24" centers, it is just a matter of time before you can drive by the house and count the rafters from your car. The OSB will have sagged considerably between the rafters.

Beams and joists, the vital framework of a home, were made of solid wood from the time of Solomon's Temple and earlier. Today we are replacing solid wood joists, beams, and even rafters with substitutes fashioned out of multiple layers of plywood (also referred to as engineered or manufactured lumber). Unlike solid wood floor joists, these are built out of two-by-fours. Solid two-by-fours make up the top and bottom of the joists with short two-by-four diagonal and vertical blocks, attached with gusset plates, providing strength.

An even more common substitute for these vital floor joists (which support the floors of the home, see Figure 5–2 on page 56) is basically thin OSB (⁷⁄₁₆"), cut to varying widths (9½", 11⅞", 14"), turned on edge, and labeled with brand names such as "Can't Sag" I-joists. You may be confused, thinking you've misinterpreted the above description of what is replacing 2"x10" and 2"x12" solid Douglas fir joists. No, you heard right. Using ⁷⁄₁₆" OSB turned on edge sounds scary and is scary.

I recently received a call from a customer with a new home which I estimate cost approximately $180,000. In other words, above the average cost.

He had called me to come and look at the home's basement that had been left unfinished. He wanted an estimate to finish the basement. As I was measuring the basement I noticed the joists supporting the first floor (probably the second floor as well) were these "Can't Sag" I–joists. In my conversation with the customer I discovered he had some degree of mechanical knowledge so I asked him what he thought of these floor joists supporting the house. His brow wrinkled immediately as though I had touched on a topic of concern to him. He said, "You know, I was worried when I noticed the builder using them, so I went to him with my concern. The builder told me they were fine. But now, when my wife and I walk across the living room floor upstairs, it feels like we're 'out on the sea'."

Another example of serious defects in new home construction is linked directly to these "engineered lumber" components.

Someone I know built a nice looking, new, two-story home which was very elaborate relative to today's standards. I would estimate its cost to be between $200,000–275,000. His wife and himself had only been in their new home one year when he asked me to come look at his exterior walls. When he had leaned against one, it felt as though it could have collapsed. It sounded serious to me and I was there the following day to investigate while the owner was at work.

The house looked impressive and no one would have ever guessed the hidden trouble. I went to the part of the home the owner had indicated. The house was sided in beveled cedar siding with a 4-inch reveal (see Figure 6–1 on page 64). I pushed against the siding and indeed it felt like I was going to go right through to the home's interior. When this type of wooden siding is used, a sheathing (backing) is required underneath it for a foundation and stability. Obviously, something was terribly wrong with the sheathing. The siding itself looked fine and was painted. I began removing the courses of siding and the problem was immediately evident. Oriented strand board (OSB) sheathing had been used and the painter failed to caulk the corner boards (vertical 1"x4" trim) where the siding abuts against them before the paint was applied. Water had seeped in at these trim boards, migrated back behind the plastic house wrap, and virtually destroyed the OSB sheathing. It was crumbling and there was nothing left to support the cedar siding. What's more, as I walked around the house pushing on the walls I found the problem affected much of the home.

I want to point out that in the old days (approximately 1950's and earlier) the lack of caulk at these same areas on a home would have had no serious consequence. In fact there are numerous old homes and apartment houses here in Iowa City (and I'm sure elsewhere) whose trim boards haven't seen caulk in years, but they are still standing plumb and level. Even if water invades these areas, there are solid wood sheathing boards to protect the structure. It would take years for any serious damage to occur. In the case I've mentioned, though, in less than one year the home's exterior was devastated.

I did not relish the duty of giving the customer this unpleasant news when he came home from work. I explained the situation and that the damage was not limited to the one small area of the home, as he had thought. Actually it covered much of the house walls.

Even though I tried to mitigate the damage and solutions to it, we were talking major repair. I explained that we could pull off all the siding, replace the sheathing with exterior plywood sheathing, and re-side the house with cedar. With the size of this house, I roughly estimated the cost to be around $25,000. As an alternative, I proposed pulling off siding that had weak sheathing behind it, replacing those areas of sheathing, re-installing the old siding, and then applying new vinyl siding to the home's exterior, for about one half the price.

The customer was devastated and rightly so. He said, "You know, Greg, the wife and I thought long and hard before investing the money and building this house. It was a big deal. Our main reason for doing it was because we were tired of doing maintenance on the other place. We wanted to do some traveling and enjoy life for a while without the burden of fixing up the home. I told her if we built a new house it would be years and years before it would require any upkeep." It was hard to deliver this news to the customer—all due to the poor quality OSB sheathing.

This newer, wooden, composite-type building material is more economical with minimal waste, but I believe that wood is best used in its natural state. Chip, slice, or saw it and glue it back together and you have a completely different product. I understand the need for forest conservation and that the use of wood (like fossil fuels) as we know it has to end. But even though we saw both of these shortages coming years ago, a substitute for either wood or fossil fuel is nowhere in sight (an exception is vinyl siding). So we continue to construct houses out of materials that apparently satisfy the engineers, but the durability of which is, to say the least, questionable.

I see examples of inferior building structures due to poor quality materials almost daily. These newer homes simply cannot go any length of time without meticulous care and maintenance. Not all maintenance situations are as dramatic as this rotted sheathing case, but many are—and these OSB problems are the type that will manifest themselves in 10–20 years in more and more abundant numbers. Part of the reason for this is that the older a home (typically, that is) the less maintenance and care it receives.

Though I've focused my criticism mainly on 4x8 feet sheets of plywood, paneling, particle board, and oriented strand board, I can by no means let solid wood boards escape notice. This includes 1x2's up to 1x12's and 2x2's up to 2x12's in all types of wood which pretty much covers all the solid boards available today at the local lumberyard. In the past you could count on finding good quality boards with appropriate moisture content at the independent lumberyard in your hometown. It was fine wood and, yes, it came at a premium price. Then the business of lumber began to change. National discount chains like Menards and Lowes began to appear and compete heavily with the independents. The quality of their wood was poor, but do-it-yourselfers didn't know the difference and the financial lure for many contractors was overwhelming. BUT you could still go to the independent lumberyard and get quality material.

Sadly, that situation is changing here in Iowa City and I suspect elsewhere. In the last year the quality of material at the independent lumberyard is nearly indistinguishable from the discount chains. I suppose they had to compromise to survive. The boards are typically of poor quality with cracks, cups, and curls. Overly wet boards are common. They stack nice and look good till you take them home and the air can reach all four sides. Then they dry, twist, warp, and bend and it becomes more and more of a challenge for the carpenter to try to build something decent out of them.

Want to step out on the deck for some fresh air? Not if your deck is constructed of "treated" (CCA) lumber. ("Just Say NO to Wood Treated with Arsenic," <u>Organic Gardening Magazine</u>, July/August, 1999, pg. 12) This is the green lumber treated with chromated copper arsenate. Toxicologists tell us even small amounts of arsenic, when ingested or inhaled over a prolonged period, can cause chronic arsenic poisoning. The "treated" lumber is touted as being rot-resistant, repelling insects and fungi. Manufacturers of this wood product say it is safe. They cover themselves legally by printing warnings for the workers at the lumberyard who saw the wood. They recommend wearing a respirator face piece, goggles, gloves, and coveralls when cutting the boards. The coveralls should be removed immediately after cutting is completed, bagged in a plastic container, sealed, and laundered as soon as possible (almost sounds like the protective gear used by medical personnel when dealing with the Ebola Virus). A veterinarian told me of a farmer whose eight 1200 pound steers ate the ashes of a few pieces of CCA two-by-fours that he had burned. It killed all eight steers. Autopsies showed acute arsenic poisoning.

In addition to CCA lumber's potential health hazard, the quality of the wood is very poor. It is typically southern yellow pine saturated with the CCA chemicals. As I mentioned earlier, wood cannot be as wet as this and still be sound. You build a deck and it looks fine. Three months later, the weather has dried it out and the result is disastrous with cupping, twisting, and warping commonly appearing. The drying process will actually dislodge a 16-penny (3" long) nail, which leaves the nail head protruding above the board's surface by ½" or so.

Many towns and cities have local building codes that require exterior construction such as staircases, decks, or wooden handicap ramps to be built either of cedar, redwood, or CCA lumber. Since CCA lumber is the cheapest of the three, it is also the most used. I shudder when I see a toddler playing on one of these CCA lumber decks.

In many ways, the home construction business is a scandal today. It is not unusual for me to receive calls for work requiring major, sometimes structural, repairs on homes less than ten years old. It seems the general decline of quality in consumer items has spread to home construction. I think that's a first for our country.

In older homes, financial limitations might be apparent in smaller room sizes, reused ¾" sheathing boards on walls or roof, fir flooring, and so on. But we find nothing that compromises the strength or longevity of the home. With new homes today, we find economy beams of questionable strength, flimsy OSB sheathing, siding of the lowest possible quality, and shingles that wear out in as little as ten years.

Hurricane Andrew revealed the shoddy construction of homes in Florida. The homeowners were devastated and local building inspectors ran for cover. Americans watching the situation unfold in Florida took it to be an isolated phenomenon, a case of unethical inspectors and builders in that particular part of the country. I wish this were so. Being deceived on a pair of tennis shoes or a VCR is one thing, but a defective house is, indeed, major fraud.

For the average family, their home represents security purchased by many years of work. If you are in the final years of your home mortgage, ready to retire, what do you do when you discover your home is falling apart?

In the late 1990's, I bought and remodeled a house that was over 100 years old. It was an interesting project. The house was not a fancy one, yet the quality of the construction and materials far exceeded that of the average home built today. This house stood level and plumb with what I suspect was minimal upkeep for decades. I believe two classes of people unwittingly avoid the trap of poor quality new homes. One is the wealthy individual purchasing the grand old home in a distinguished neighborhood. The other is the middle-class individual who cannot afford to build a new home and settles for a modest older one. They are both luckier than they know. My own home is 30 years old. Anything newer and you start seeing the construction quality wane.

I am not condemning builders. If a builder insists on better quality materials than are normally used, he will price himself out of the market. To reverse the reprehensible trend towards cheap construction materials, customers need to be made aware that they are buying poor quality homes and what the consequences may be. Armed with this knowledge, they will then demand that better quality materials be used. The market for better quality materials will then have been created. I hope this book will contribute to the development of that trend.

In the meantime, my advice to people who are health- and quality-conscious is to look for homes of a 1960 or earlier vintage. If, however, you want to design and build your own home, but do not want it loaded with the cheap materials used today, I have a possible solution. Negotiate with your builder to dismantle an old house and re-use the lumber. This may sound radical at first thought, but not rightfully so.

Scores of derelict homes exist in both rural and urban settings, some of which can be obtained without charge in return for removing them from the property. The wood in these homes is excellent. It is of a distinctly higher grade than is commonly available today and also is superbly dry. I am referring to the old two-story homes. They contain a great deal of lumber and to build a new average-sized home would require only a minimal supplement of new materials. I cringe when I see a bulldozer leveling an old home, as though we had trees to burn. This is quite simply mindless waste.

Let's say you purchased an old two-story home for a nominal cost of $5,000. I would estimate that a four-man crew of carpenters could dismantle and clean up the lumber (remove nails) in three to four weeks. Based on a $20/hour/man cost, we could estimate $12,800 for labor plus the $5,000 purchase fee, giving a figure of $17,800. Add to that figure $4,000 for siding (which is hard to salvage in the dismantling of the home) and we have a grand total of $21,800. The lumber cost of a new home today generally ranges between $30,000 and $50,000.

Here's a thought! Some new homes today are built with a 19th century flare: old-style porches, steep roof pitches, etc. These features may seem a little incongruous in that the houses are also "modern" with thin brickmold window casings, aluminum storm doors, a lack of ornate work, and, though not apparent, poor quality materials. There are old carpentry books around, complete with designs and plans of homes built decades ago. Why not dismantle these otherwise useless homes in the countryside or in ghettos, and reconstruct them according to these old plans. Many people love these existing old-style homes, but they can be a liability in terms of maintenance, reasonable though this may be considering their age. Wouldn't it be exciting to own a newly built home with all the design, detail, and appeal of a 1900's house? It would be encouraging as well to know that a home built of good quality, full dimension, "recycled" lumber would require no maintenance for years. With reasonable care, your great grandchildren could be raised in this house. You would also have saved money and at the same time made a contribution to ecology.

Even if the idea of old home re-creation doesn't appeal to you, remember the advantages of buying a home of a 1960 or earlier vintage.

Let's Get Started

In the following chapters, I will accompany you through a prospective home, explaining the features to look for and beware of. Some of this information may seem obvious to you, but much of it will not. We will begin with the basic systems: electrical, plumbing, heating, and cooling. After that we will examine the basement, then look at siding, roof, attic, ventilation, etc. The last three chapters contain pertinent general information and finally, in a condensed summary, we have included an all-important checklist that is the key—our tool of discrimination when evaluating a home. Simply read this brief, concise, information-filled book to learn how to use and apply it. Also, extra copies of this checklist are located at the end of this book. Feel free to photocopy them as needed.

Chapter 2
Electrical

Chocolate Nut Brownies

I fondly remember my first house-wiring job. It was in 1972, here in Iowa City, for Nate Moore Wiring Service. Nate was rather gruff and as no-nonsense as his bib overalls. He did, however, show his compassionate side in taking me on when he really wasn't looking for additional workers. Nate's expertise in electricity was unsurpassed. I used to listen as three or four master electricians discussed some electrical puzzle, looking for the proper solution. Nate would pass by, catch about two sentences, declare the answer, and never miss a step. He was something.

My training began with wiring service panels, a very tedious task that entailed standing in one spot on a concrete floor meticulously connecting wires to breakers for what seemed like forever to an eighteen year old. I did it well and was consequently stuck with that job for months. I think it was Melrose Market, a small grocery store/bakery that shared the building with Nate Moore Wiring Service, that helped me through those 'service panel' days. I still remember their delicious baked goods, especially the chocolate nut brownies, oven-fresh every Friday morning.

Electrical Basics

The following basic information on house wiring should give you a better understanding of the guidelines offered in this chapter.

Let's begin at the utility pole. The electrical cables coming to a home are called the 'service drop'. If there are two wires, 110 volt electricity is available. A third wire is necessary to provide 220 volt service. Most homes have 220 volt service in the form of a twisted, three-strand drop (tri-plex). The service drop connects to the service head on the outside of the house. From there, the wires travel down a conduit, pass through the electric meter, and continue into the service panel (see Figure 2–1 below).

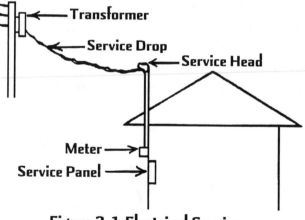

Figure 2–1 Electrical Service

There are two basic service panel types: fuse and circuit breaker. Opening the cover on a fuse-type service panel will reveal several round fuses and one or two pull-type "main" fuses. The "main" fuses in a fuse-type service panel are ordinarily located near the top of the panel with the individual circuit fuses (round ones) located below (see Figure 2–2 below). Opening a circuit-breaker service panel door

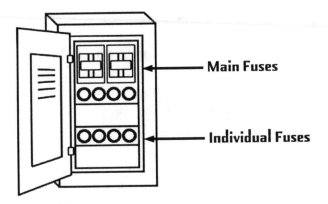

Figure 2–2 Fuse Type Service Panel

will reveal a "main" breaker (black switch) at the top of the panel and either one or two vertical columns of individual circuit breakers (black switches) below (see Figure 2–3 on following page).

From the service panel, the electricity goes out into the home. The amperage to each circuit is determined by the size of fuse or breaker controlling that circuit. If you use an appliance that requires

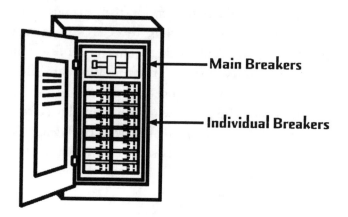

Figure 2-3 Breaker Type Service Panel

more amperage than the fuse or breaker can provide, as a safety device the fuse will blow or the breaker will trip and break the circuit.

The size or capacity of the service panel determines how much electricity is available in the home. This size, in its turn, is determined by what voltage is coming from the transformer outside. Years ago, when electricity was first introduced into homes, 15, 30, or 60 amp levels were the norm, since electrical appliances were rather limited. Electric lighting was common, but required relatively small amperage. In 1972, when I began wiring for Nate, a 100 amp service was considered sufficient for most homes. But as we continue to be pampered with more and more electrical luxuries, the need for a larger amperage level of service has grown. Today, a 200 amp electrical service is not considered excessive.

To find the amperage size of an electrical service panel, simply look at the "main" breaker located at the top of the panel. The capacity will be marked on the lever portion of the "main" breaker. The amperage size of a fuse-type electrical service panel is also indicated on the "main" fuse(s). Occasionally two fuses (side by side) at the top of the panel serve as the "mains". If there are two "main" fuses, the capacity of the service is the combined sum of the two.

Before concluding this brief course on electrical service basics, I want you to learn the difference between a grounded and a non-grounded outlet.

Non-grounded outlets are a potential hazard. They also indicate old wiring. They are probably fed by a fuse panel (inferior as compared to the breaker-type service panels) and one of an inadequate size at that. A non-grounded outlet has two sets of two-pronged female receptacles. The outlet has one "feed" or hot wire, one neutral wire, and no ground wire (see Figure 2–4).

Figure 2–4
Non-grounded Outlet

A grounded outlet has two sets of three-pronged female receptacles. The outlet has one "feed" or hot wire, one neutral wire, and one grounded wire (see Figure 2–5).

**Figure 2–5
Grounded Outlet**

A Further Note About Electricity: Some Do's and Don'ts.

1. If you are unfortunate enough to have a fuse box or fuse-type service panel, do not play the old trick of placing a penny behind a fuse that keeps blowing, thus bypassing the fuse altogether! This is asking for trouble because when a fuse is continually blowing, it indicates problems with the circuit—usually a short. Bypassing the fuse allows the short to heat up, which might lead to a fire.

2. Though this may seem obvious, it is worth restating. Home owners should not allow handymen or anyone other than a licensed electrician to do electrical work. Most city codes demand this. Still, I've seen a lot of "cobbled" electrical work obviously not done by a professional.

3. Do not stand in water or even on wet ground or anywhere near a sink or tub full of water while operating an electrical device. Electrical outlets near the kitchen sink or anywhere in the bathroom are dangerous if they are not ground fault outlets (which include an electrical interruption device). If there is common contact with both an electrical device and water, the body rivals the grounding system of the house, directing voltage and (more importantly) amperage through itself. Ground fault outlets are an excellent safeguard against electrocution and shock and should be used in bathrooms or near kitchen sinks. They should also be used in exterior outlet locations. Though high electrical voltage is obviously dangerous, cardiologists now tell us that in susceptible individuals low-voltage shocks (such as common house current) can induce fibrillation, a serious interruption in the heart's rhythm and pumping ability.

4. Make sure your aluminum ladder or any other piece of conductive material does not come into contact with your service drop wires. This is particularly important if your wires are old and of the single strand type (two or three wires). Even if you have the newer, twisted, three-wire type (tri-plex), you should still avoid contact as described above, though generally there is no risk of death. With a tri-plex service, you have two heavily insulated lead wires and a bare,

neutral wire. The only danger is that of a mild shock due to static electricity coming from the neutral wire on a wet day. Cardiologists might still regard this as to be avoided.

5. Familiarize yourself with the "main" breaker or fuse in your service panel. Pulling out the "main" fuse in your fuse-type service panel will disconnect all power to the home. "Throwing" the "main" breaker in your circuit-breaker-type service panel will do the same. The reason for having one switch ("main") to disconnect all power to the house is to make it possible to act speedily in case of an emergency such as a short or flood water.

What to Look For

Bear in mind that a fuse box or fuse-type service panel is an outdated service control for the home. It is severely limited in terms of circuit number capacity and also in terms of amperage capacity. It is also somewhat dangerous when it comes to changing fuses.

The two-wire service drop is a serious defect. Remember that if the house has a circuit-breaker service panel and grounded outlets, it is unlikely it will have a two-wire drop (simply count the wires in the service drop to distinguish between two and three wires).

However, if the house does have a two-wire service drop, it can be corrected for a few hundred dollars, the amount depending on the conduit, service head, etc. present. All that may be required to bring the system up to standard is a tri-plex service drop.

If, on the other hand, the house has non-grounded outlets and a <u>fuse</u> box, this is a critical defect. The cost of rewiring such a home may run into several thousand dollars.

If the electrical service capacity is below 100 amps, again, this is a critical defect. Specific cost to correct this situation depends on what related deficiencies exist, such as small service wires, inadequate transformer at the pole, and general poor condition of the interior wiring. A low amp service level is usually associated with one or more of these deficiencies.

Ideally, What You Want to See Is:

◆ Tri-plex service coming from the pole.

◆ Grounded outlets.

◆ A breaker-type service panel, with 100 amp or greater capacity.

Chapter 3
Plumbing

The water service and waste water systems for homes in the country are complex. Since the vast majority of people live in a town or city, it is urban plumbing we will describe in this chapter. Residential plumbing is generally built to last and is not a common source of trouble requiring maintenance or replacement. The key word here, though, is generally.

Types of Water Supply Lines

Water service usually comes into the home by way of a ¾" or 1" galvanized pipe through the basement wall and into the water meter. Utility people no longer need enter the home to read the meter as its figures are relayed to an auxiliary meter on the exterior of the home. Water leaves the meter, traveling through distribution pipes that are usually between ⅜" and 1" in diameter. The commonly used types of plumbing supply pipes are not equally good, as will be discussed below. Typical plumbing supply lines used in residential plumbing are plastic, galvanized iron, or copper.

Plastic

Plastic water supply lines are not generally recommended. There is some question as to a plastic line's tolerance of water pressure, even at levels commonly used in homes. There is also debate as to whether or not the polyvinyl chloride (PVC) the pipes are made of leaches into the water. PVC is a known carcinogen when the body absorbs its fumes, either through the sawing of PVC pipe or the burning of PVC material. You will recognize this pipe by its plastic appearance and white color.

Another concern with PVC water lines is whether the glued joints will hold up. They have not been time-tested. With the widespread use today of plastic pipes (because of the ease of use and low cost), wouldn't it be a disaster if the glue compound broke down in, say, 15 years? In view of the high cost of replacing them, I would advise against a house with plastic water supply lines.

Galvanized

Galvanized iron water pipes are another common type of water line seen in residential plumbing. The primary shortcoming of galvanized pipes is the tendency for the pipe's interior to corrode. If the pipe is corroded, its capacity is reduced and consequently water pressure is diminished. The results are, among other inconveniences, a weak shower stream, inadequate garden hose pressure for watering, and the annoyance of waiting forever for a sink or tub to fill.

To replace galvanized pipes would be a major undertaking, costing several thousand dollars, and a big inconvenience. I would strongly advise passing over a house with galvanized pipes in the absence of a water softener system and in the presence of low water pressure. While copper pipes are colored like pennies (some bright, some tarnished and darkened) and are extremely smooth, usually approximately ½" in diameter, galvanized pipes are larger (approximately 1" in diameter), their surface is somewhat rough, and the color ranges from silver to black. Galvanized pipes are acceptable if there is a water softener and the water pressure is good.

Copper

Copper is king. Copper pipes are superior in that they do not corrode, rust, or otherwise wear out. They are also known to be a healthful water conduit, provided lead-based solder was not used to join the pipe sections.

EPA regulations banned the use of lead-based solder in June 1986, as it was discovered that lead had been leaching into the tap water (states were given until June 1988 to comply). Testing for lead contamination and solutions are discussed below. Provided a water softener and a drinking water purification system are included in the home, lead is not a concern and copper lines are rated as the first choice for water supply regardless of the solder.

Testing for Lead and Other Contaminants

Everyone should have his/her water tested for the presence of lead and other contaminants. Many times the municipal water system may be a source of lead contamination long before the water reaches the home. To determine if the lead source is in the home's pipes, turn on a tap and immediately take a water sample. Then allow the water to run for a couple of minutes and take another sample. Have both samples tested for lead. If the first sample is positive and the second negative, the home's pipes are the source of the lead. If both samples are positive, the city pipes or a combination of the city pipes and the home's pipes are the source. If both samples are negative, of course, there isn't a lead problem.

Though lead in drinking water is a concern, there are solutions to the problem. Detection of lead need not disqualify a prospective home. If the source of lead is the pipes in the home, the tap water can simply be allowed to run for a couple of minutes before drawing a drink.

Water Purification Systems

The use of a water purification system is a better solution in that it will eliminate lead, as well as many other contaminants, regardless of the source. The most effective water purification system combines a drinking water filtration system, a water softener, and a whole-house pre-filter system.

A carbon-filtration or reverse osmosis drinking water unit will remove inorganic health hazards such as arsenic, barium, cadmium, chromium, fluoride, lead, mercury, nitrate, and selenium. Smaller units (under the kitchen sink) for drinking and cooking water only are the most popular and practical. A reverse osmosis unit, which costs around $750, provides the best system, in practical terms, available today. It is strongly advisable to have a drinking water purification unit in your home whether you have lead soldered pipes or not, in view of the myriad of poisons and carcinogens present in our nation's water supply today.

I consider a water softener to be a mandatory home feature, though it is to some degree a matter of personal preference. Often a common fixture in the basement, a softener treats the home's entire water supply and removes the mineral hardness caused by iron, calcium, and magnesium. The removal of these minerals helps prevent corrosion in the water supply pipes as well as aiding in other areas of home operation and maintenance.

Some water is so saturated with natural and man-made hardness and contaminants that drinking water purification units cannot process it. Softened water reduces the workload of the drinking water purification apparatus (reverse osmosis, carbon filtration, etc.) and increases its efficiency. It will also extend the life of the RO membrane in a Reverse Osmosis water purification unit.

Softened water is also much kinder to appliances, such as the clothes washer and humidifier, in that it does not leave behind mineral deposits that can decrease efficiency and reduce appliance life. (Using softened water for laundry also facilitates cleaning, reduces the need for soap, and helps extend the life of clothing.)

Another good example of the benefit of softened water is the hot-water heater. Hard water will continue to leave mineral plaque on the inner tank of the hot water heater, progressively diminishing its capacity. It has to run more often than normal to keep up with the demand for hot water.

If I haven't sold you on the importance of a water softener yet, how about those difficult bath tub rings? I would insist on a softener if only to prevent those.

Carbon-based, whole house pre-filters that remove dirt, sediments, and some contaminants such as chlorine are available. These also lighten the load for the water softener and drinking water system.

Drains

Drain sizes are commonly 3–4" for main drains and 1–2" for sink and tub drains. They are usually made of cast iron, plastic, or copper. Copper, again, is best. Copper drains in a home are a definite sign of high quality construction. Plastic, being so much cheaper than copper, dominates. In new construction, cast iron is pretty much obsolete. In older homes, cast iron drains are the rule. When it comes to drain lines, the specific type is not as critical as in supply lines where water pressure is a factor. Thus plastic drain lines are acceptable. All that it should really be necessary to ascertain in your inspection of the home's drains is whether or not they are draining properly.

What to Look For

The first concern should be water pressure. Check sinks and tub(s) for adequate volume of water flow. **If the flow is small, taking an unusually long time to fill the sink or tub, this is a critical defect.** Whether the problem is corroded pipes or undersized ones, correcting it is a major undertaking.

When checking for pressure, note the color of the water when the tap is first turned on. Brown or red tints in the water can also indicate excessive corrosion in the lines. Checking for this sign of corrosion in galvanized lines is vital. I have removed old lines in homes on remodeling jobs and found them to be nearly full of build-up. A water softener would have prevented these pipes from corroding by removing the calcifying minerals in the water. If there is no softener, you should pass on this particular home.

While it is relatively inexpensive to install a water softener, its absence in combination with galvanized pipes is cause for concern. Even if a water softener is present, verify that the galvanized lines are not clogged to an unacceptable extent by checking for adequate water pressure. It cannot be assumed that a softener has been in continual use since the house was built.

Plastic water supply lines constitute a critical defect. You would be faced with the questionable safety of the drinking water and the possibility of having to replace the lines at some future date.

Be sure to check the drainage of the sinks, tub, and stool. They should drain quickly and the stool should flush well, completely clearing the bowl. Look under the sink and see if the curved drain trap is leaking. Traps do rust through in time and, though this is not a grave concern, it may indicate maintenance neglect on the part of the present owner. If the supply lines are good but the drain lines are slow, a major plumbing problem is not necessarily indicated. This situation would, however, warrant an inspection by a plumber. The problem could simply be a clogged drain line. Conversely, it could indicate something more serious such as a high spot in a main drain line under the basement floor. These high spots are not unheard of and deter the gravitational emptying (flow) of the drain.

As mentioned before, a water softener is, in my view, a must. It extends the life of appliances, protects pipes from corrosion, and removes mineral hardness from the water. It also increases the efficiency and life of drinking water purification units. And, as we have seen, its installation does not entail a great deal of expense.

Though hot water is certainly mandatory in a new home, I do not consider a faulty hot water heater a major problem. In fact, for a relatively small price ($400-500) a new, high efficiency, sealed combustion hot water heater can be installed that will save money in the long run and which will also not allow carbon monoxide (CO) into the home (see Chapter 10, page 110).

Ideally, What You Want to See Is:

♦ Good, strong water pressure.

♦ Copper lines as both supply and drains, or other acceptable pipes, providing water pressure is good.

♦ A functioning water softener.

♦ Drains, working properly.

♦ No obvious signs of leaking pipes or plumbing in disrepair.

Chapter 4
Heating and Cooling

Several types of residential heating systems are currently available. We will focus on the type that almost completely dominates in home placement—the forced-air gas furnace.

A solar-, water-, or electric-type heating system is not necessarily a disadvantage, but unless you are experienced in the field of engineering, you are unlikely to be able to judge the quality or efficiency of these less-common types. I have included my brief impressions of these three systems.

Solar— A solar system is a good source of supplemental heat and probably has great potential as a clean, renewable, and environmentally safe source of primary heat for homes. At present, however, it is too unrefined to be a practical alternative.

Water— A water system is touted as a healthy type of heat, but the technology has not kept pace with electric or gas heating technologies. Water heat lacks the simplicity of the gas furnace in both operation and maintenance.

Electric— An electrical system is also regarded as a healthy, clean type of heat. The cost, however, can be prohibitive.

The Forced-Air Gas Heating System

The gas furnace is an excellent heating system with an abundant fuel supply. The newer models are extremely efficient and, as a rule, require no maintenance other than changing the air filter once a month.

Incidentally, if you have a forced-air gas furnace and are not changing the filter every month, you should be. Allowing the filter to become clogged with dirt will not only contaminate your household air, but it will put additional strain on the furnace's blower motor dramatically reducing its life.

Though your house tour inspection of the furnace will be limited, it is a vital part of your overall inspection of the home. Don't expect to have every furnace in every home you look at inspected. But when you find a good home that passes your personal preliminary inspection of the furnace, it is time to have the furnace professionally inspected, if possible. This is important, particularly with regard to health concerns.

Among other things, the heating professional will look for cracks in the heat exchanger. Though this is uncommon (it would render an old furnace useless), a cracked heat exchanger will allow carbon monoxide to infiltrate the home with potentially lethal health risks to the inhabitants. The fact that the current owner is alive and in good health would, of course, suggest that the heat exchanger is sound. Nevertheless, a professional inspection is warranted. If you do buy the home, you should have the furnace cleaned and adjusted.

I would not recommend bypassing a nice home if the furnace is found to be defective. If the furnace needs replacing (approximate cost of $2000 for an average home), it would provide an opportunity to install a high-efficiency furnace in a house that is otherwise in good shape. Federal law now requires new furnaces to have at least a 78% annual utilization efficiency rating (AUER). With an older furnace's AUER being as low as 60% or less, the advantages of replacing it with a newer model with a 90% (+) AUER are obvious. The replacement should pay for itself in a matter of several years and pay dividends thereafter.

What to Look For

Determining the existence of a central air conditioning unit should be a primary concern, although this will, of course, depend upon the climate in your region of the country as well as your personal taste.

If you do require a central air conditioner and the prospective home is without one, this would obviously constitute a serious defect. The cost of a good central air unit is roughly $2000, providing furnace ductwork exists to accommodate the unit. I should add that large shade trees are under-recognized today as to their home cooling value. Old carpenters tell me that several decades ago good quality shade trees were a vital consideration when building new homes. Air conditioning, of course, has diminished the need for shade trees. However, with the current awareness of energy conservation and the threat of chlorofluorocarbons (new EPA regulations are phasing out the old chlorofluorocarbon refrigerants), the planting and nurturing of shade trees is highly desirable. (The EPA placed a total ban on the production of chlorofluorocarbons effective June 1, 1996. However, manufacturers could continue to use existing inventory.)

While a well-known brand name is no absolute guarantee that the unit is in perfect condition, it does let you know that you have a quality product. Familiarize yourself, therefore, with the following brand names: Lennox, Trane, Rheem, Carrier, Rudd, and York.

Ask the real estate agent to operate the thermostat to engage first the furnace and then the air conditioner while you are standing near the units. Note the sound of each unit. Ideally, you want to hear a smooth-running motor without grinding or rattling noises.

Another prudent step, if you are seriously interested in the home, is to ask the realtor if recent utility bills are available from the current owners. Depending on your local gas and electric company's policy, they may be happy to provide you with a particular home's average utility bill over the preceding 12 months. This option is available here in the Iowa City area.

Finally, scrutinize the furnace and central air unit for obvious signs of age or disrepair. Is the furnace sitting in a quarter inch of water with heavy rust? Do the units look like antiques?

Ideally, What You Want to See and Hear:

♦ Furnace and air conditioning units that look well maintained.

♦ A well-known brand name on both units.

♦ Smooth operating noises.

♦ Confirmation of reasonable utility bills.

♦ Well-established shade trees.

Chapter 5
The Basement

Driving Rain, Children, and Floods

It was November, 1992, and my wife Deb and I were involved in a marathon enterprise—moving to a "new" home. Of course, our children were a big help, especially the two-year old and four-year old. Psychiatrists tell us that moving is second only to losing a loved one as far as major life stressers go. But I don't think they factored in children, driving rain, and flooded basements. You know the feeling that comes once you have completed a difficult task? That tired but satisfied sense of well-being? After carrying in our last load of boxes, we were able to enjoy that feeling for probably all of three minutes—until I walked downstairs to admire our new, beautiful, and **FLOODED** basement!

The basement had been a nice feature of our new home, with finished walls, an oak bar, an additional kitchen, and $2000 worth of high-quality carpeting. But the sump-pump motor had failed.

When a carpeted basement is flooded, the water has to be extracted immediately. If the three-or four-day process of drying out the carpet is delayed, the carpet will be lost to mold. Deb and I were ready for therapy. Careful as we had been in our inspection, nature and chance had conspired against us. (Read on for advice on preventing this dilemma.)

Basement Basics

For me, a basement is mandatory. However, if the basement shows noticeable moisture or wetness, all it amounts to is a place for stored items to mold or rust. There are techniques for waterproofing a basement to reduce or eliminate floor water, such as the "Beaver System". However, these techniques do little to deal with high humidity levels in the air. Even if you are willing to pay for dehumidifiers, empty or drain them, and endure the noise, they are no match for a highly humid basement. A wet or damp basement is letting water or humidity in through the walls or the floor. This may be due to cracks in the floor or walls, improper grade work (described in Chapter 12, page 129), or an inadequate foundation drain.

A foundation drain is a perforated tile conduit that follows the perimeter of the house along the bottom of the basement wall. It rests on pea-rock (a smooth rock resembling peas in size and shape) or sand and collects water. When the pea-rock cannot absorb all the water, the foundation drain carries it to the lowest corner of the house to a well or holding tank known as a sump pit. When the water level in the sump pit reaches a designated level, a pump in the pit forces the excess water either into your yard or into the storm sewer, averting a wet or flooded basement.

The problem that caused our flooding was a burnt out sump pump motor that had allowed the pit to overflow onto the basement floor. I replaced the motor and also installed a "stand-by" sump pump powered by a 12-volt battery that will take over in the event of a failure of the regular sump pump. A battery powered sump pump stand-by unit is simply an additional pump that sits in the pit alongside the conventional sump pump (see Figure 5–1 below). It provides good protection and can be installed for a couple of hundred dollars. Had a stand-by sump pump been installed in our new home, it would have

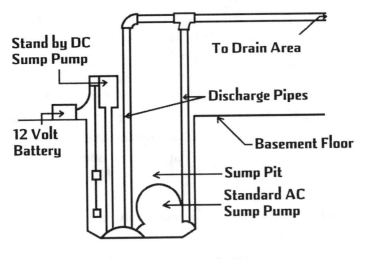

Figure 5–1 Sump Pit, Pump and Stand-by Unit

prevented the flooding we experienced. It is also a good protective measure in the event of a power outage. Generally, standard homeowner's insurance will not pay for flooding due to a faulty sump pump, or for any flooding other than that due to faulty indoor plumbing.

Hairline cracks in a plumb basement wall, without bulges or depressions, are not necessarily a concern, particularly if the home is 30 years old or older. On the other hand, bulging walls, large cracks, or wet or moldy walls indicate movement. As I point out in Chapter 7 on Foundation and Structure, movement is rather like a slow-growing cancer in its effect on the overall health of the home.

The basement floor is important too. I should mention that it would be good to see floor drains, particularly in the laundry room. Also, look for intact floors without cracks or signs of movement. However, large cracks or signs of movement in a basement floor are not nearly as common as cracks in the walls, because basement floors are well below the frost level and are therefore more protected from movement. Nevertheless, in certain conditions such as sub-grade shift of earth or basement water infiltration, damage can occur to the basement floor. Sub-grade soil with a layer of clay between layers of sand can encourage earth movement, though usually the builder or engineer has ruled this out. Another example where earth movement can occur would be a home simply built too close to a hill or steep bank that is eroding.

If the basement floors are carpeted or covered with vinyl, your floor inspection will be somewhat obstructed, but you should still check for any depressions or irregularities in the floor covering. With carpet, run your hand across it to check for dampness. Also, put your nose right up to it and check for a musty smell. The home may have been sprayed recently with a deodorizer to mask a telltale odor.

The basement usually affords a view of the first-story floor framing (see Figure 5–2 on the following page). Of course, this is not the case if it has a finished ceiling covering the first-story floor joists. Floor joists are commonly spaced 16" apart, though they may be spaced at 24" as well. These floor joists span the entire basement from exterior wall to exterior wall, are frequently spliced together roughly midway, and are supported on either a wooden or steel beam if the span is of considerable length. If the first-story floor framing is exposed, take the opportunity to inspect for rot and insect damage. This also offers the opportunity to sight across the bottoms of the joists to check for any significant sagging.

A common fixture in the basement is a water softener and/or other water filtration system. The merits of water filtration systems are discussed in Chapter 3. As mentioned before, I consider a water softener to be a mandatory feature, though it is to some degree a matter of personal preference.

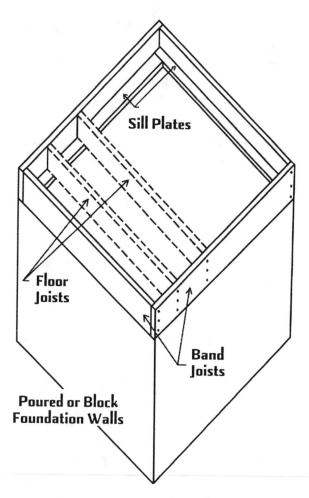

**Figure 5–2 First Floor Framing
Basement Ceiling**

What to Look For

Feeling as I do about having a dry basement, I will summarize some of my advice.   Wet or significantly damp basements are trouble. Because of corrosion, they will shorten the life span of appliances. They are unfit for storage of clothes and many other items. If you do your laundry in a damp basement and sort and hang it up there, the clothing will absorb this foul dampness.

A wet or damp basement also constitutes a health hazard. It is a strong invitation to spiders and insects, not to mention bacteria and mold. If the basement is damp, the furnace can draw this damp air if there is no door or barrier to the upstairs as return air and re-circulate it, spreading all the mold spores and contaminants it contains through the house. Even the fancy electric air cleaners available today may be hard pressed to neutralize this problem.

The cause(s) of dampness may be multiple and varied, as may be the means of correcting them, if such means can be found. I have friends who have hired contractors (basement waterproofers) with unsatisfactory results. As I said before, it may be possible to eradicate standing water, but eliminating dampness is another matter.

Sniff as you first walk down the basement steps. If you detect strong humidity or dampness, look on the bright side. You're one house closer to the one you really want. This is a critical defect.

A sump pit may be necessary, depending on your region of the country. This would hold true for any region receiving 20" or more of rain annually. Here in Iowa, as in much of the rest of the country, the need is present. However, there are houses even here which, depending on the type of sub-soil and the home's proximity to underground water tables, may have absolutely dry basements even without a sump pit. If you are looking at a house with no sump pit that is sufficiently dry and whose owner can vouch for the lack of dampness or water problems, it may be reasonably safe to assume that this is true— particularly if you are looking at the house in the spring or during a period which has seen recent rain. If a sump pit exists, have a look at it. If possible, take a bucket and pour water into the pit to a level that will activate the pump. Observe the pump for efficiency and listen to the motor.

Cracks in the foundation (basement) walls may indicate a critical defect as serious as a cracked engine block in your car. My rule of thumb is that **any crack(s) larger than ¼" are critical,** as previously noted. Of course, if you have multiple cracks measuring ³⁄₁₆" this also is cause for serious concern. **If you have several hairline cracks covered with mold which are leaching water into the basement, a critical problem would be indicated.** Look for mold or dark spots discoloring the walls. Also, look for bulges in the walls, which indicate significant movement.

Floor drains in the basement are a nice convenience, particularly in the event of water problems such as overflowing sinks or flood water.

Look at the first-story floor framing, which is, more often than not, exposed in the basement. First of all, sight across the bottoms of the joists to detect any serious sagging, which I would define as over 1" in a 12' span. Some sag is normal, especially in an older home. *If the first-story floor joists sag more than an inch, I would consider this a serious defect and proceed with a master carpenter's inspection, if you are still interested in the home.*

I would prefer that the joists be on 16", rather than 24", centers (distance apart), irrespective of how substantial the first-story flooring boards may be. Use your thumbnail (or better yet your car key or a screwdriver) and probe any joist or framing member that appears discolored or shows any signs of flaking or erosion. Pay particular attention to the exterior wall and to both the band joists and sills (see Figure 5–2 on page 56). These three areas are typically the most susceptible to rot and insect infestation. The area where the sill sits on top of the foundation wall is usually dark, so taking a flashlight along would be a good idea. Pests and insects will be covered in a later chapter.

If you do see signs of rot, depending on the extent, this would at least warrant an inspection by a master carpenter.

Look for a water softener. If the home has none, remember that it will cost about $1500 to have one installed. With regard to water softeners, I have one more comment to make. You will probably not be able to judge a softener's quality by sight, so it might be advisable to take a water sample in a small bottle. A water purification company will gladly test it for you in hopes of selling you a softener and/or purification unit. You might think this is like asking the barber if you need a haircut, but I've found several local companies to be pretty honest in their analysis. If you are concerned, however, you can have an independent lab test made. You may, of course, forego the inconvenience of testing if you don't consider the problem to be insurmountable, even if a new softener is indicated.

Another desirable amenity in your basement is washer and dryer hook-ups if they are not provided in another part of the home. Though the absence of these hook-ups might not constitute a defect, remember it will cost a few hundred dollars to have a plumber and possibly an electrician install them.

Take advantage of the exposed framing (if such is the case) of the first floor (ceiling of the basement) to look for electrical wires that seem outdated or improperly installed (for instance, having 2 feet of slack hanging from the ceiling). If you spot such wires, make a mental note.

Ideally, What You Want to See Is:

♦ In view of the information above, we'll place a dry basement at the top of our list of priorities.

♦ A sump pit, if indicated in your region of the country.

♦ Straight walls, without cracks, bulges, mold, or moisture.

♦ Floor drain(s), particularly in the utility/wash room.

♦ Clean and dry framing, with no signs of sagging, rot, or insect damage.

♦ Although not vital, a water softener.

♦ An absence of loose or old wiring in the ceiling.

♦ Washer and dryer hook-ups.

Chapter 6
Siding

Siding is of obvious importance, comparable to the roof, in protecting a structure's interior and occupants from the elements. Its primary function, of course, is to keep out wind and rain. However, to avoid difficulties in the future, two factors need to be taken into account: low maintenance and durability. This chapter will provide basic information on the common types of siding you are likely to encounter in your home search.

Clapboard Siding
(Beveled Wooden Siding)

Being a carpenter, I will begin with my favorite—clapboard or beveled wooden siding. It is also the favorite siding of many discriminating homeowners, a testimony to its high quality and beauty. If you tour the older homes in the upper class neighborhoods of your community, you are bound to see an abundance of clapboard siding. Until recently, clapboard siding was unrivaled in terms of longevity and appearance. Improvements in aluminum and especially vinyl siding have changed this to some degree.

Clapboard siding is a beveled piece of wood usually of cedar or redwood (occasionally of pine on less expensive homes). It is sold in widths ranging from four to twelve inches. The siding measures ½" to ¾" at the butt, with the ½" size by far the most common. The siding is applied to the exterior house wall in a fashion similar to shingles on a roof.

Application begins near the foundation and proceeds upward with each course of siding covering a portion of the top of the preceding course, which provides a water seal. With the siding installed, the exposed portion is referred to as the 'reveal' (see Figure 6–1 below). On older homes it is common to

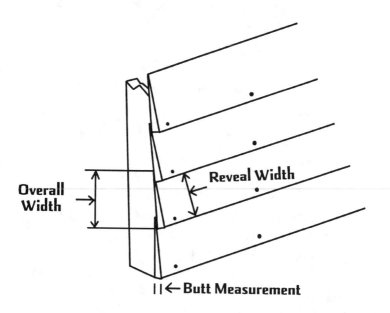

Figure 6–1 Clapboard Siding

see a reveal of two to four inches. Generally a wider variant is seen on newer homes with a five to eight inch reveal.

Clapboard siding has considerable aesthetic appeal as well as a long life. I don't believe I have ever needed to replace a rotten piece of clapboard siding, even in neglected homes nearly devoid of paint. The reason for this is because wood that can immediately and completely shed water and dry is naturally resistant to rot. If properly painted, clapboard siding will look beautiful for years. Nevertheless, to contribute to the growing effort to conserve our natural resources, especially the world's trees, all concerned homeowners might want to consider alternatives to wooden siding. As for existing clapboard siding, preserve and enjoy it.

Aluminum Siding

Aluminum siding is available in a variety of factory-enameled colors. It has the advantage of being permanent in that it will never corrode, rust, rot, or otherwise wear out. Its shortcomings, however, should be kept in mind. Although improvement has been made in designing aluminum siding to look like wooden clapboard siding, in my opinion it still falls far short. Even if wood is not the targeted look of a particular aluminum siding, you still do not want it to look like a cheap metal covering on the home. Unfortunately, it often does.

Secondly, aluminum siding is dangerously susceptible to marring and denting from children's play, ladders set against the house, and hail. I have seen a home's aluminum siding completely ruined by a single hailstorm and, although insurance may cover this damage, the inconvenience of having to replace the siding is something the homeowner would probably prefer to live without.

Vinyl Siding

Carpenters of the past will probably turn in their graves, but I have some positive things to say about this plastic impersonator! Vinyl siding is a flexible, plastic siding, usually designed to mimic clapboard siding, with approximately a 3" reveal. The better grades of vinyl siding retain their color, the plastic itself being solidly colored before the siding is cast. This insures a constant color unaffected by superficial, external damage. Better grade vinyl is supple and resists drying out or becoming brittle. I can also vouch for its attractiveness and near perfect replication of the appearance of wood siding. Vinyl siding is unsurpassed when it comes to maintenance— provided it is professionally installed, it <u>never</u> requires any.

Cedar Shingle Siding

Cedar shingle siding has its merits and demerits. Appearance could fall under either heading, depending on personal taste. As far as maintenance goes, it is comparable to clapboard siding if it is painted professionally. Alternatively, it can be left unpainted as it is naturally resistant to rot and is nearly maintenance free. If left unpainted, it will weather to a medium brown (antique look) which may or may not be to your liking.

Generally, cedar shingle siding is a low maintenance, durable, quality siding.

Asbestos Siding

Asbestos siding is composed of individual pieces of asbestos-fiber-impregnated cement shingles measuring approximately 12" x 24" x ³⁄₁₆". There are two basic styles of asbestos siding shingles. They have similar dimensions with one having a straight bottom, the other wavy (see Figure 6–2 below). Since

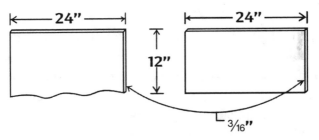

Figure 6–2
Common Styles of Asbestos Siding

asbestos shingles are no longer available, non-asbestos replacement shingles are available today to restore the home if a shingle is broken or missing. Lumber yards usually either stock or can order them. As you will learn later in the roof chapter, asbestos roof shingles are a cause for concern. However, if they look good and are intact, asbestos siding shingles should not necessarily be considered a defect. We are aware today of the dangers associated with asbestos dust, but the risk exists only if the shingles are broken or otherwise disturbed which creates dust. Simply having asbestos siding covering a home is not a threat in itself.

Asbestos shingle siding is long lasting and low maintenance. Though should you desire to replace the siding, the cost (see Chapter 8—The Roof, cost to remove asbestos shingles on page 88) and inconvenience (the necessity of leaving your home for a few days) should be considered.

Brick Siding

Brick siding is of exceptional quality, both durable and attractive, provided it is in good condition with no evidence of cracks or movement. If the grade work is properly carrying water away from the foundation, the gutters are intact, and the brick's mortar joints are in good shape, there is no maintenance required on a brick home's exterior walls.

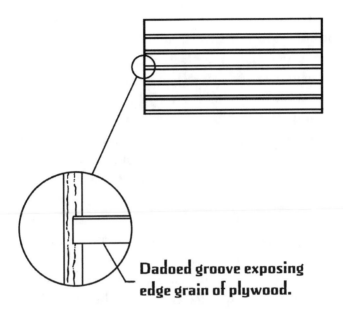

Dadoed groove exposing
edge grain of plywood.

Figure 6–3
T-111 Shown Horizontal
Vertical When Installed

Vertical Plywood Siding

Vertical plywood siding, referred to as T-111 (see Figure 6–3 above), is simply a plywood sheet bonded together with exterior grade glue. It is four feet wide and comes in lengths of eight and nine feet. It is typically ⅝" thick and available in cedar and fir, with fir being the most common. It has grooves plowed out on either 4" or 8" centers to mimic the look of separate solid vertical boards.

The problem with T-111 is that plywood does not hold up well as house siding despite the exterior grade glue used to bond it together. The plowed grooves expose the weather-sensitive edge grain of the plywood creating the potential for de-lamination, which is extremely common. Once de-lamination begins, the house must be re-sided. Paint companies have not helped this situation because they encourage the preservation of T-111 with a semi-transparent stain, a highly diluted oil stain that virtually disappears within a couple of seasons. I believe the stain is inadequate to begin with because of the lack of full-bodiedness and sealing qualities. Furthermore, homeowners will naturally be reluctant to recoat their home, as would be needed, every two or three years. The selling feature of the semi-transparent stain is that it does not hide the natural beauty of the wood siding. The paint stores, however, neglect to tell you to buy it by the car load, because you'll need to re-coat the house almost continually.

Let's say you just bought a brand new home with bare T-111 siding. If you primed it with oil and applied two coats of a high-quality oil- or water-based paint, you would have a good finish that should last approximately ten years. However, a problem arises when you buy a home that has already had various finishes applied to the T-111 siding. You cannot be sure that what you want to apply will be compatible. In other words, you may have cohesion problems which will result in peeling paint. So, in my opinion, T-111 (vertical plywood siding) should be avoided.

Masonite/Hardboard Siding

Masonite (brand name) or hardboard (generic name) siding is a composite siding bonded together with heat and adhesive. Its most common dimensions are 12" x 16' x $\frac{7}{16}$". It is designed to be installed horizontally with each course overlapping the preceding one by an inch or so, similar to clapboard siding after which it is patterned. Unfortunately, it is nowhere near as long lasting as clapboard siding.

Trouble usually manifests itself in areas where paint is thin or entirely gone and water infiltrates the siding causing swelling and deterioration. A particularly susceptible area is where nails have been driven and unintentionally countersunk, leaving a small dimple where water will set. Carpenter's hammers have heads that are convex to assure that with the last blow of the hammer the nail is set flush or even slightly countersunk. That is a desirable effect when the carpenter is nailing wood, as is usually the case. In general, he nails the hardboard siding as though he were nailing wood, which leads to this problem.

Hardboard siding frequently deteriorates, as has been happening on my home. When I purchased my home, the hardboard siding was one of the defects I overlooked because of the home's other qualities. Sometimes this siding will last thirty years; sometimes not nearly that long. The last time I purchased Masonite brand hardboard siding for a repair job, the clerk at the lumber yard insisted I sign a manufacturer's waiver. The waiver stated a provision that I would not use the material outside! Doesn't say much for the company's confidence in its product, does it? I don't care for hardboard siding, but then it is not an insurmountable obstacle. Three to four thousand dollars should cover that hardboard with a nice vinyl siding, if the rest of the house checks out.

What to Look For

Though clapboard siding is top of the line, it should be kept in mind that it does have a maintenance requirement. Assuming the paint coating was kept in good shape in the past, it should require only a pressure washing, spot priming on bare areas, and high quality, exterior grade paint applied every ten years or so. *If, however, the paint appears checked, thick, and missing in places, these are telltale signs of past amateur paint jobs and you should be aware of the potential expense of two to three thousand dollars to restore the exterior walls.*

A word of warning about rough-sawn clapboard siding: Its roughness is a problem. It doesn't look good painted with a full-bodied, heavily pigmented, quality paint. **Furthermore, if it is painted with this type of paint and requires scraping at a later date, the roughness and softness of the siding will render this practically impossible.** The only alternatives are either to preserve the natural color by coating it with the semi-transparent stain every few years or by letting it naturally weather to an antique gray color, which may not be what you want.

If the house has aluminum siding and you are none-the-less still interested, check for excess paint dust on the surface. Lower quality and older styles of aluminum siding were designed to shed superficial layers of paint over the years to continually provide a fresh look. The problem is this continual layer of dust creates a dull, lackluster appearance. It also eventually culminates in areas of bare or near bare aluminum and creates problems with new paint adhesion should you want or need to repaint the home. Check also for a pitted surface such as that caused by hail. If aluminum siding is unacceptable to you, remember that it is widely recommended that old aluminum siding be removed before applying, say, new vinyl siding. **I believe dusty or pitted aluminum siding constitutes a critical defect.**

Though an on-site chemical analysis of vinyl siding cannot be done, some practical steps can be taken to look for quality. First, its appearance should be acceptable. Beyond that, look for cracks. Also check, by pushing against the siding, for extreme rigidity or a lack of flexibility. Each piece should flex as you push it and then assume its former shape. Pushing against the siding should also give you an indication of whether or not it is securely attached to the house wall. I have seen homes with poorly attached siding or poorly fitting joints that would have been apparent had a walk been taken along one exterior wall while 'spot' pressing the siding.

Though I would not seek out a house with asbestos siding, I wouldn't totally avoid a house sided with it. Check the walls for cracked, broken, loose, or missing shingles. Many times asbestos shingles on homes have never been painted and the factory color is lime green or another off-color. Commonly, the siding is white with unsightly stains or mold. Take heart. Though asbestos siding is very absorbent, it paints up well. An oil-based primer plus 2 coats of a high-quality house paint is recommended. I should also point out that this paint treatment will add moisture and flexibility to this old siding, breathing new life into it.

A brick home's exterior walls are of exceptional quality providing there has been no wall or foundation movement and also providing the mortar joints are sound. **Information on checking for foundation movement is covered in Chapter 7— Foundation and Structure. An examination of the foundation is extremely important, though movement in exterior brick walls is a critical defect regardless of the cause.** Movement would be indicated by cracks in either the brick or mortar joints significant enough to disrupt the right angle checkerboard pattern of the bricks. Also check the mortar joints for soundness by digging at them with a key or screwdriver. **If the mortar erodes easily, consider this a critical defect.** This condition would require a mason to replace the outer ½ inch or so of the mortar (tuck pointing) and could cost in the neighborhood of three to six thousand dollars depending upon variables such as single- or two-story house, depth or erosion of mortar, and so on.

T-111 and Masonite siding have relatively short lives. *If the home you're considering has either T-111 or Masonite siding, this is a serious defect. There is at least a possibility that the home will need to be resided in the not-too-distant future.*

Ideally, What You Want to See Is:

♦ Clapboard siding, smooth paint without cracking or peeling.

♦ Aluminum siding, dent free and without excessive dust.

♦ Vinyl siding with a pleasant appearance that is supple and firmly attached to the house walls.

♦ A brick home with sound mortar joints and no indication of exterior wall movement.

Chapter 7
Foundation and Structure

The All Important Foundation

As might be expected, the foundation of a house is of vital importance to its general health and longevity. It is my foremost concern when I'm sizing up a house, even though I suspect the average homebuyer pays little attention to it. The foundation's soundness is vital to the structural quality of the home. Structural defects are nearly always related to foundation problems. Exceptions to this would be the case of under-engineering or gross neglect of the structure's siding or roofing to the point where the interior of the building was exposed to the elements. Pest damage occasionally causes structural defects as well.

A very slight amount of movement in the foundation is normal over the years. But I must stress that it would have to be <u>slight</u>. Movement significant enough to produce ¼" and larger cracks in the block, concrete, or mortar is a matter of grave concern (more on this later).

Function of Foundations

The foundation's function is to provide a solid, immovable base on which to attach the home. The depth of the foundation walls depends on how far frost extends into the ground during the winter months, if frost does occur in your part of the country. Ground above the 'frost line' will move, ground below the 'frost line' will not. The idea is to have a portion of the wall extend below the 'frost line' to serve as an anchor to hold the entire foundation wall secure. In Iowa, we like to go three to four feet deep because frost rarely goes deeper than two feet here. In the warm southern areas of the United States 'frost footings' are not required, although foundations are commonly placed down several inches to provide lateral stability. For buildings in the extremely cold parts of the world, such as at Arctic and Antarctic scientific outposts, 'frost footings' are not a concern either. Frost there extends into the ground hundreds of feet and is referred to as "perma frost". Since it never thaws, there is no movement. Houses with basements have foundation walls extending well below the 'frost line.'

Types of Foundations

The relatively rare types of foundations will not be discussed here. Instead, we will concentrate on the three types of foundations found in the vast majority of homes: block, brick, or poured concrete.

There is some debate as to whether brick and block are superior to poured concrete. It is true that a poured foundation reinforced with steel rods is stronger, but a good block or brick foundation wall is also more than sufficiently strong. Both will develop hairline cracks in time and I suppose the block wall has an advantage in that it will drain exterior moisture or water downward through its hollow core, rather than allow water into the interior of the building. However, neither has a significant advantage over the other.

Structural Problems

Cracks indicate movement in the foundation. Usually the problem lies outside the building, in the grade. The grade should slope away from the building, carrying water away from the foundation. It is as important a factor as rain gutters in preserving foundation integrity. If water is allowed to pool next to the foundation, it will repeatedly freeze and thaw, having the effect of a hydraulic press between the ground and foundation that produces movement and cracking.

Cracks and movement in the foundation produces problems-a-plenty. Once movement begins, it is usually progressive. Problems range from poor fitting doors to gaps in the siding to misaligned gas and water fittings. Invariably, movement in the structure will let the elements in compounding the problem. Homes will pass from owner to owner as the defects manifest themselves. I've worked on houses with this problem and it seems that every time I pass by there's a new realtor's sign stuck in the yard.

What to Look For

As you walk through the home, close a few doors and check them for fit. With the door closed, note the margin between the door and the jamb, both on the side of the door with the handle (strike side) and the top of the door. This distance should not vary greatly. Site along the strike side of the door from the floor to the head jamb, and along the top of the door from side jamb to side jamb. A small variance is common, particularly in a house thirty years old or older, but not to the point where the door won't close or allows daylight through when it is closed.

Look for cracks in the plaster or drywall at the top corners of the door casings. These also are acceptable and not uncommon if they are hairline cracks and the house is over thirty years old. If a house is less than thirty years old and doors fit poorly or cracks in drywall are present at the tops of door casings, additional inspection of the foundation is indicated.

If floors and walls lean so much that it is evident to a non-carpenter, this is not acceptable. **Badly sloped floors or leaning walls may or may not be linked to a foundation problem, but none-the-less** indicate a structural problem and constitute a critical defect.

Foundations are not always visible. Sometimes they are covered on the exterior of the home by the siding. In a finished basement, the foundation is hidden from view in the interior of the home. If possible, examine the foundation, even if it requires squeezing through a scuttle hole into a crawlspace. More often, you will be able to view a fair portion of the foundation from the exterior or in the form of a basement wall from the interior. **If a foundation/ basement wall has cracks ¼" wide or larger, has significant depressions or protrusions, or has obviously been patched or repaired, this is a critical defect.**

Foundation mortar, the cement holding the block or brick together, should appear intact and should not crumble if you dig at it with your fingernail. **If the foundation mortar is missing or weak and powdery, this is a critical defect.**

A reasonably good test of the general structural health of a home is to simply stand back and view the exterior perimeters. **The vertical corners of the home should appear plumb. The roof line and foundation line should appear level. If not, this is a critical defect.**

Occasionally, you will see a home whose foundation is visible from the exterior only and it has the look of stucco or smooth mortar. Many times this means that a veneer layer of Portland cement has been applied to the block or brick to support and hide cracks and movement. If such is the case, this is a critical defect.

Ideally What You Want to See Is:

Exterior

- House appears to set level and plumb.
- Straight planes across the roof with no unusual depressions.
- Any exposed foundation looks intact with no large cracks or sloppy areas of repair.

Interior

- Reasonably level floors.
- No leaning walls.
- No large cracks in plaster or drywall at tops of doors or doorways.
- Doors that close properly.

Chapter 8
The Roof

War and Roofs

Despite the lure of the brownies at Melrose Market, I began to experience a growing boredom with the electrical trade. It was repetitious work, either standing at a service panel or on my knees wiring outlets, fishing wires through conduit, or crawling through an attic. I couldn't imagine doing only this type of work until I retired (my respect for those who do). Carpentry intrigued me, as I think it does all men to some degree. The satisfaction of building something out of wood is considerable and, with that desire in my heart, off I traveled to Centerville, Iowa. I had learned of a master carpenter there named Lloyd Shinn, a fellow Welshman, who agreed to hire me and train me in carpentry. Lloyd, like Nate, was an exceptional man in his field. He was also in excellent physical condition. In his late fifties, he could have passed for thirty-five. His complexion was smooth and tanned and he had the muscular build of a college boy with what looked like about a thirty-inch waist.

One of our first projects was the complete remodeling of an old farmhouse several miles outside of Centerville. Among other things, the roof of the home needed to be replaced. It had a build-up of several layers of shingles and was extremely steep. The work was physically exhausting, though Lloyd worked right alongside four other "grunts" and myself. The "grunts" muttered sounds of displeasure while I wondered about my move to carpentry. It seems that jobs like these always have to be done in July, and as the sun was cooking the sweat out of us, Lloyd called for a break under a maple tree in the yard. The homeowner's gracious wife also took pity on us and sliced us a platter full of tomatoes from the garden. During the break, Lloyd told us an old war story with the goal, I believe, to somehow convince us we were actually fortunate to be there on the roof rather than fighting Japanese, for instance!

The battle for control of the Philippines was a relentless one. Lloyd and his company had been on the move for ninety-three days. Their sleep came in half-hour naps while in full combat uniform with mortar and rifle fire all around. Lloyd and his fellow soldiers could feel their feet bleeding from time to time as it had been days since their boots were off. It was at this point that the company commander bravely offered some humor to boost his men's morale. He said he had some good news and some bad news. The good news was that the next day they were to get a change of underwear. The bad news was that Shinn was to change with Johnson, Gilbert was to change with Lewis...and so on. Back up the ladders we went, spirits renewed.

Roof Basics

Several types of roof systems will be discussed in this chapter, although you should keep in mind that in the U.S. the asphalt-shingled roof is by far the most common in about the same proportion as the forced-air gas furnace is for heating.

Asphalt Shingles

The asphalt shingle measures approximately 1' x 3' and has an inner membrane covered with an asphalt outer layer and finished with a surface of granulated minerals (small rocks). It is applied to the roof with each shingle overlapping a little over one half (7") of the preceding shingle to cover the nail heads. An adhesive strip located in the exact area where the shingle will be nailed permanently seals

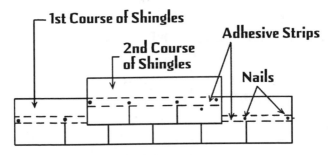

Figure 8-1 Sealing Illustration

(holds down) the edge of the succeeding shingle (see Figure 8–1 on the previous page).

Asphalt shingles may either be hand-nailed, air-nailed, or air-stapled. The air method is a highly efficient one, requiring just a fraction of the time needed to hand nail. In the air method, a pneumatic gun powered by an air compressor fastens the shingle to the roof with a galvanized staple or nail. A common <u>misconception</u> exists that shingles applied with either a pneumatic stapler or nailer are inferior to those that are hand-nailed. The newness of the process scares some people. Others are convinced the method must be shoddy if it is that much faster than hand nailing. This reminds me of stories my father told about how skeptical people were when power saws first became available. I guess carpenters hung on to their handsaws for some time. Anyway, regardless of these attitudes and of hearsay beliefs, air-applied asphalt shingles are just as good as hand nailed. In fact, pneumatic staples may be superior to hand-driven nails due to the fact that the staples are resin coated and they bond to the wood into which they are driven. A carpenter friend of mine said it well, "Once the shingles are sealed (by the adhesive strips), you could throw the nails away." This statement is true.

I recommend Certainteed brand "custom" shingles for an expected life of twenty to thirty years. Standard off-brand shingles today wear out in ten to fifteen years, despite their twenty-five, thirty, or thirty-five year guarantees.

Wooden Shingles

Cedar (wooden) shingles, either the thinner, smooth type or the thicker, rougher looking hand-split "shakes," have a nice appearance, but are becoming less popular. The main reason for this is cost. However, another reason is the scarcity of shingles that have been adequately dried. Cedar shingles that contain more than the proper amount of moisture will cure on the roof, usually leading to cupping or curling. If this occurs, they need to be replaced.

Copper or Aluminum Shingles

Copper or aluminum roofs are fine and I would recommend them highly if you were building a new home that you planned to live in for many years. They are maintenance free and last virtually forever. The cost of aluminum and copper roofs can be respectively five to ten times as expensive as asphalt shingles. However, I would caution a homebuyer against buying an old home with a copper or aluminum roof that may have been painted, coated with various roof protective substances, or otherwise improperly maintained or modified. These situations may be impossible to correct.

Slate Roof

Slate roofs are fine, but like copper or aluminum, they are extremely costly. Slate is a natural stone, typically mined in the eastern United States. A problem that slate has in common with asbestos shingles is that invariably, over the decades, there will have been traffic across the roof and the brittle shingles will have cracked or broken. Cracking or breaking also occurs due to adverse weather conditions as well as simply with time. Replacing slate shingles is tricky and not inexpensive.

Asbestos Slate Roof

Asbestos shingles are a slate-type shingle, approximately ¼" thick, and composed of Portland cement and asbestos fibers. They are no longer sold. Most roofs covered with them are old and the shingles are cracked, broken, and have missing corners or whole shingles missing. Most homes with existing asbestos shingles are due for re-roofing. The shingles are old and broken and often are letting in water. The problem here is the cost. Since asbestos is known to cause lung cancer, it is a big concern with government health and safety agencies. The crew that removes the asbestos shingles either has to be certified by or comply with the regulations of the EPA (Environmental Protection Agency), OSHA (Occupation Safety and Hazard Administration), DNR (Department of Natural Resources), and both the Federal Clean Air and Toxic Substances Control Acts.

The cost alone of removing an asbestos roof can amount to $200 or more per square (that is 100 square feet). You are looking at a removal cost alone of over $4000 for an average-size home.

What to Look For

If the home you are considering has an asbestos roof, this is a critical defect.

If, on the other hand, the home you are looking at has wooden shingles that are mold free, crisp, and straight, and there is no interior evidence of leakage, it would probably be safe to assume the roof is adequate. *If you see any signs of mold, decay, holes, cupping, or curling, I would be concerned and consider this a serious defect.*

I would consider a slate or metal roof to be a serious defect though it may actually be sound. The problem is, you won't know, and even finding an expert to evaluate them may be difficult. So, in order to protect yourself and in the absence of a professional to assess the quality of these uncommon roofs, I would pass on them.

An asphalt roof is really what we want to see. It is not going to last forever, but then again the cost of re-roofing an asphalt roof is reasonable and it lacks the hidden dangers and uncertainties of the other types.

Though not absolutely critical, it would be worth knowing how many layers of shingles the roof has. Shingles overlap by approximately half their

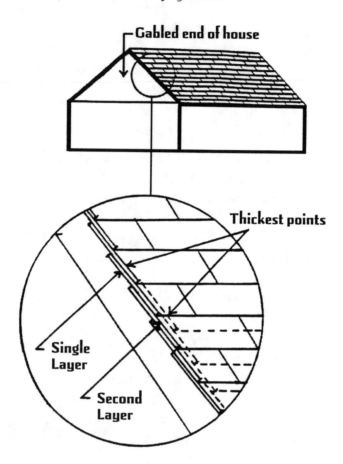

Figure 8–2
Determining # of Layers of Shingles

vertical height (see Figure 8–2 above). To determine
the number of layers of shingles on the gabled end
of the house where shingle edges are exposed, count
the number of shingle layers at the thickest point
and divide that figure in half. A pair of binoculars

works well for this. If the prospective home has a hip-style roof (no gables), you will need a ladder to inspect the edge of the roof at the eave (by the gutter). Again, count the number of layers and divide in half.

Common building practices and codes allow shingling over one existing layer of shingles without compromising the structural integrity of the home. As a rule, two or more layers of shingles should be removed before new shingles are applied. The cost of shingling over an existing single layer of shingles on an average size home would be roughly $1500. To remove two layers of shingles on a home and then apply new shingles would cost roughly twice that amount. *Cupping, curling, significant depressions, or erosion of the mineraled surface constitute serious defects in an asphalt shingled roof. It is a serious defect, also, if your prospective house has over two layers of asphalt shingles.*

Flat roofs and skylights are frequent sources of leaks. Carpenters have long known that any roof surface that does not quickly shed water or that allows water to stand (flat or low slope roofs) will leak. It will be a constant source of aggravation and will need ongoing maintenance, though it is true that the new rubber roof systems are a dramatic improvement over what has been available in the past. Skylights, if top-of-the-line grade and professionally installed, can be leak free. However, it is hard to determine if this is the case. **If a prospective home has many skylights, if a good-sized area of the roof is flat or** low slope, or if a combination of both situations exists, you can either look forward to a long and meaningful relationship with a local roofer or you can eliminate this house as a candidate for your future home.

Ideally, What You Want to See Is:

◆ One or two layers of asphalt shingles.

◆ The mineraled surface of the asphalt shingles still present with no bare or eroded areas.

◆ No cupping or curling of the shingles.

◆ Straight planes as you sight across the roof with no unusual depressions.

◆ No evidence of leakage/damage in the interior of the home.

Chapter 9
Insulation and Attic Ventilation

Most homes built in 1960 or later are insulated and supplemental insulation can be added. Homes older than 1960 that are not insulated or adequately insulated can be insulated and brought up to standard. So this chapter will not detail any situations that would elicit any defects—critical or serious. Rather, it will simply provide incidental information for you in sizing up a home.

Insulation in the home provides a barrier through which heat and cold find it difficult to pass. The basic idea is to keep warm air in and cold air out of the house in the winter. Of course, insulation works to do exactly the opposite in the summer (providing you air-condition your home). As basic information, the common types of insulation will be described. Then we will go on a short educational tour of the basement, main floor, and attic to show what types are used where and how they are used appropriately.

First, let me define, in rough terms, the often-heard phrase, R-factor. R-factor simply refers to the insulating capacity of a particular product or its 'R'esistance to heat or cold passing through it.

Insulation is used in most parts of the US, particularly for cold-proofing homes in the northern part of the country and heat-proofing homes in the South. The more extreme the conditions, the more insulating power needed. That is to say, a higher R-factor is indicated. To get an idea of just how much R-Value is needed for your specific area, refer to Figure 9–1 on the next page.

The more common types of insulation are described below.

Fiberglass Insulation

There are many forms of fiberglass insulation, most of it sold in rolls cut to common stud and joist spacing widths. Thicknesses include 3½" and 6¼" for walls and up to as much as 13" for attic applications. Some brands are faced with kraft paper and others with a plastic vapor barrier. Others have no facing and are referred to as friction-fit since they are simply pushed into place and held by their snug fit in the prospective cavity. 'Faced' fiberglass insulation is typically stapled into place.

Vermiculite

Vermiculite is the white, light-weight, pebbly material that is also sold to lighten and better drain soils in flower pots and the garden. It is blown or sometimes poured into stud and joist spaces.

Figure 9–1 R-factor Map and Ratings

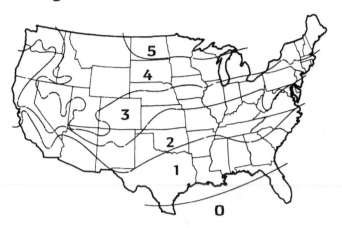

Insulation for Winter Heating

	Minimum	Maximum
Zone 1	—	R-19
Zone 2	R-11	R-38
Zone 3	R-11	R-49
Zone 4	R-19	R-57
Zone 5	R-19	R-66

Insulation R-factors are noted in above zoned map. Match the zone to the chart. Also, note Figure 9–2 R-ratings of Different Materials on the following page. Even air space has some insulation qualities. Those residing in Zone 0 need some insulation for air conditioning. The amount can vary. Check with your insulation retailer for the right amount.

Source for Figure 9–1 and 9–2: HWI Hardware Store pamphlet

Figure 9–2
R-ratings of Different Materials

Material	R Rating
Air space (per inch)	.94
Gypsum wallboard (½ inch)	.79
Hardboard (¼ inch)	.20
Plywood (¾ inch)	.93
Asphalt shingles	.44
Plastic vapor barrier	trace
Padded carpeting	2.09
Common brick (4 inch)	.85
Concrete block (8 inch)	1.1
Floor tile	.04
Sheet/sprayed plastic foam (per inch)	5.0
Polystyrene boards (per inch)	4.0
Polystyrene sheet (per inch)	4.0
6 inches unfaced fiberglass insulation	19.0
3½ inches unfaced fiberglass insulation	11.0

Wool

Wool insulation looks like little fuzzy pink pebbles and, like vermiculite, is blown into place.

Foam

Foam insulation is typically a urethane-based product that is injected into the stud spaces of a home through holes drilled in the exterior walls.

Rigid Styrofoam

Panels of rigid styrofoam are available in varying thicknesses and sized to accommodate stud and joist spaces and other applications.

All these types of insulation are generally good ones with the exception of the roll-type fiberglass faced with a vapor barrier and the urethane foam type.

First, let's talk about why I don't recommend fiberglass insulation faced with a vapor barrier. Vapor barriers are recommended in walls and attics to keep warm, "moist" air from passing into the wall cavity or into the attic; meeting cold air at this 'dew point,' and condensing, causing the insulation to become wet and useless. This wetness, in theory, could also cause damage to the studs, siding, and sheetrock.

As a carpenter, I've never encountered any example of this dreaded moisture condition causing the insulation to become wet nor have I ever seen the subsequent rot or damage in the wall cavities. I believe you would have to be continually boiling several caldrons of water in the home with an almost arctic temperature outside to produce this situation—at least as far as the walls go. I don't know if this is just a misguided engineering theory or perhaps a premise to accommodate a sales market (plastic sheathing).

I haven't encountered damage due to the lack of a vapor barrier. However, I have seen numerous examples of damage due to its use. I've received calls from customers perplexed at mold growing on walls and ceilings, usually during the winter months with the furnace operating and cold temperatures outside. The mold is usually in a bathroom, kitchen, or near a humidifier. The moisture in these areas needs to escape to the outside and is prevented by the plastic vapor barrier in the wall or ceiling. I believe this moisture would escape safely and gradually in the absence of a vapor barrier with no damage to insulation or wall structure.

In fact, a friend of mine here in Iowa City has a ventilation/insulation company. When he contracts to do a whole house upgrade, his first priority is to send men to the attic to cut all insulation vapor barriers with utility knives. He would do the same to any insulation vapor barriers in the walls if they were accessible.

I also have an objection to the use of urethane foam. It is usually pumped into stud spaces through holes drilled in the outside walls of the home. Marketing claims include a high R-value, durability, and a property of being able to fill any size or shape void. In other words, it can completely fill any given area, leaving no space through which air can pass from the interior to the exterior of home or the reverse.

The problem with foam insulation is in its long-term durability. I have torn into old walls in homes insulated with foam in which the foam has almost always shrunk over time leaving a space of ½" to ¾" around the entire perimeter of the cavity it once filled. This, of course, is like having a boat with holes in it. Not good. Also, the foam has typically lost its integrity, crumbled, and settled or has cracks in it. Manufacturers claim the foam will not deteriorate if not exposed to light, but I have not found this to be the case.

I realize this information on insulation may be too detailed and technical to interest some readers. However, I have included it for those people who want to understand the insulation matter more completely and in more depth. Now, let's take a tour of the home.

Basement—Unfinished—Unheated

Most basements are heated so this example will be an exceptional one. If the house has an unheated basement or, in the absence of a basement, an unheated crawl space, it would be a good idea to insulate the underside of the first story floor. This would be done by installing 6¼" fiberglass insulation faced with a vapor barrier (here a vapor barrier IS good to keep moisture OUT of the home) or styrofoam panels with a plastic vapor barrier applied over the finished product. Note that if a crawl space exists, it should be ventilated. Vents and installation advice are available at your local lumber yard.

Basement–Unfinished–Heated

In a heated basement, we are not concerned with heat penetrating the walls since it cannot do so to any degree. Nor are we concerned with heat flowing up and through the floor as this is no loss to the overall house. The only place where a heat loss is experienced in this situation is at the band joists or the perimeter of the basement walls (at the top ten inches or so, see Figure 5–2 on page 56). To insulate these areas, cut 10" or 12" strips of 6¼" fiberglass insulation with kraft paper facing and staple onto the band joists.

Basement–Finished–Heated

When looking at a finished basement in a prospective home, we will not be able to determine if the walls are insulated or not nor will we be able to modify or add insulation. But, for the sake of your knowing, I will describe the appropriate wall insulation treatment used in finishing a new basement.

First of all, the ceiling is not a concern. We do not need to insulate it as heat lost to the upstairs is a benefit to the home. So, we simply construct whatever type of ceiling is preferred, without insulation. The exception might be if we wanted to soundproof the ceiling to isolate (sound wise) the basement from the first floor. If such was the case (basement equals playground for children), a special sound control fiberglass insulation would work well.

The walls are an important matter. When constructing exterior walls in a basement, there are two basic methods. One is to attach firring strips (either 1x2's, 1x3's, or 2x2's) to the brick, block, or cement walls. The problem with this method is that you are limited in how much insulation you can get in this small space. With 1x2's or 1x3's, you only have ¾" and with 2x2's you have 1½" of space. Insulation, either ¾" or 1½" styrofoam panels, are placed snuggly between the firring strips. Then a 6 ml plastic vapor barrier should cover the entire wall area before the walls are finished with sheetrock or whatever is being used. Like in the crawlspace, a vapor barrier IS good here as we are trying to keep OUT moisture and basement walls can tend to be damp or emit moisture. I should also say here that prior to finishing any basement, a definitive determination should be made as to adequate dryness. I've seen finished basements that have water problems and the walls are a moldy mess, full of unsightly stains and, in time, deterioration.

Another problem with attaching firring strips to the walls is that the finished wall will mimic the basement wall (block or cement) in irregularity. There may be slight bulges or depressions and the wall may not be straight.

Alternatively, let's consider a 2x4" wall built just like the ones upstairs. It's superior in several ways. We can get more insulation in it (3½" of fiberglass) and you can hold the wall far enough away from the exterior wall (block or cement) so as to construct it straight. Again, after the studs are up and the wall is insulated, apply the plastic vapor barrier before any wall finish.

First and Additional Floors

Chances are you will be unable to determine whether or not the walls of a prospective home are insulated. A carpenter, either through removing an electrical outlet cover and peeking past the electrical box with a light or through peering down stud spaces in the attic, may be able to detect insulation in the walls. As I've mentioned, it is not uncommon to find older homes devoid of insulation. In the old days a fuel shortage didn't exist and there was no need for energy conservation.

For me, a home's lack of insulation is not a concern. Not that I am careless with my money. I just have strong feelings about homes being over-insulated and too tightly closed up with house wraps. I've bought homes both with and without insulation and have never added insulation to the homes that had none. That is with the exception of the attic which I will detail later. I realize I am unique in this attitude of unconcern over a lack of insulation in a home. I just think an uninsulated home is healthier than an overly tight home.

Most of the older homes that lack insulation are of the vintage that used solid ¾" sheathing boards under the siding, usually clapboard. This is quite a barrier to drafts in itself and it has somewhat of an R-value, especially when the dead air space in the wall is considered in addition to the typical 1" or so of plaster on the interior walls. I bought an older home like this and left the walls uninsulated. I did, however, restore the caulking around the windows (windows are a significant source of heat loss) and installed new, tight storm windows. I also added blown insulation to the attic and the house was very comfortable with utility bills that were reasonable.

So I wouldn't be concerned if you are unable to determine the wall insulation status of a prospective home. Even if you're not as unconcerned as I am in that regard, you can always add insulation if you prefer.

The Attic

On the subject of attic insulation, we will also include information on ventilation as it is related. Again, some of this information will be pertinent to your inspection of the home, some you may simply add to your growing comprehensive home knowledge.

If possible in your inspection of the home, look in the attic. It may be revealing. Most homes have a step ladder around somewhere and I'm sure the realtor wouldn't mind your using it. First, make a general visual inspection. Hopefully the rafters will look good with no cracks or water damage. Give attention to the underside of the roof surface as it may contain damage that is not evident from an exterior view. However, the damage described above is rare.

Let's get to the insulation. The rule for the amount of insulation in the attic is "a lot," as this is the major site of heat loss in homes. As you know, heat rises and it tries desperately to go up through the attic. An ideal attic would have 6¼" of fiberglass insulation and an additional 6–8" of blown insulation on top to further insulate and fill all the cracks and voids. An attic is relatively easy to insulate, so there is no need to panic if insulation is inadequate there. On the other hand, it would be nice to see insulation in ample amounts.

We need to talk about attic ventilation. Again, this information is not exclusively for the inspection, but I believe every homeowner should understand this aspect of home mechanics as it is an important one.

First of all, we need to understand this basic concept which totally bewilders most people. Our objective in attic ventilation is to try to get the air in the attic as close to the outside air temperature as possible—winter and summer. In the summer, if heat is trapped in the attic, there is an oven sitting on the home causing undue stress and work for the air conditioner. And in the winter months in areas where it gets cold and snows, if there is inadequate attic ventilation, heat from the home will escape up through the ceiling (unlike the walls) in sufficient amounts to actually create that damaging moisture when it hits the dew point. That point (where hot meets cold and condensation occurs) many times is at the roof sheathing and consequently ice can form on the shingles of the house. Usually the ice forms towards the eaves or edges of the roof as the insulation there is commonly the poorest in terms of a good seal.

So, good attic ventilation is of paramount importance and adding it to a home is not monumental either in trouble or cost. I defer to the local contractors and lumberyards to give you specific advice on the appropriate types of attic ventilation as recommendations vary according to attic sizes, styles, roof pitches, etc.

Ideally, What You Want to See Is:

♦ Ample attic insulation (the particular type is not critically important) hopefully reaching to the tops of the joists.

♦ Realize also that a home that lacks ample attic insulation is a situation that is easy and relatively inexpensive to correct.

Chapter 10
Pests, Carbon Monoxide, and Radon

Pests

Though recommendations for specific pest inspections and treatments are, to a degree, region-specific, termites and carpenter ants are the primary concern and their damage can be found in homes in much of the United States.

Although they resemble white ants, termites are actually more closely related to the cockroach. The primary food source for termites is cellulose, a carbohydrate found in wood (as well as other plants). Though termites can survive on grass, organic ground matter, and trees (particularly decaying ones), wood in homes is not unattractive to them.

Carpenter ants are black and quite large. The queen can be an inch long. They are very vigorous, seeking out old wood, logs, stumps, and standing-dead trees as homes. It is thought that carpenter ants eat wood, as do termites, though actually they only chew the wood to form nests. While they seem to prefer dead wood, we know that they also inhabit healthy trees (damaging or killing them) as well as lumber in homes.

The fear of termites and carpenter ants is disproportionate to their actual occurrence. Many banks do not even require a pest inspection before lending money on a house. It is not unusual, however, to see a pest inspection requirement on a purchase agreement. With pest control companies graphically advertising the destructive potential of these insects in the yellow pages, it is not surprising that the prudent homeowner would be concerned. Probably the most likely person to uncover termites or carpenter ants is a carpenter when pulling off siding, tearing out walls, etc. I've worked on hundreds of remodeling jobs over the years and have found carpenter ants maybe a dozen times and termites only once.

Still, although an infrequent occurrence, when termites and carpenter ants are present in the home, we obviously have a problem. There may be few signs of infestation and in many cases even pest control companies fail to detect these pests. Usually, it is the damage they cause that is the first sign of termites or carpenter ants.

Moisture within the house structure is conducive to, if not absolutely necessary for, infestation by termites and carpenter ants. A leaky roof is commonly the culprit. Water will remain between the shingles and sheathing or run down a wall and provide regular moisture for the insects. Another source of moisture would be around the foundation or around poorly maintained windows (improper caulk maintenance). Any cracks around windows or doors (exterior) or wet or rotted siding should alert you to the need for an inspection for pests. Your interior inspection should be focused on the basement or crawlspace. Look over the floor joists and particularly the band joists and sill plates (see Chapter 5, page 56). These first-floor structural members are usually the primary location of insect damage because of their susceptibility to wetness and their proximity to the ground from where the pests migrate. Take along a flashlight and screwdriver and thoroughly inspect and probe, especially towards the ends of the floor joists (near the foundation). Also look for any little piles of sawdust, a common evidence of carpenter ant infestation. If you examine both the exterior and interior of the home and find it to be in good shape and lacking any pest markers, I would consider a professional pest inspection optional. If, however, you do find evidence of termites and/or carpenter ants, a professional treatment by a pest company will be indicated. Additionally, repairs by a carpenter to remove any damaged wood, as well as corrective measures to insure all sources of moisture are eliminated, are indicated. Provided the damage is not extensive, a home's previous infestation with termites and carpenter ants should not eliminate the home from consideration.

Carbon Monoxide

Carbon monoxide (CO) should not disqualify a prospective home as it usually does not involve a major expense to eradicate. Nevertheless, it is a concern and the furnace man should carry out testing for it when he checks the furnace. Should you buy the home, I would also recommend that a CO tester (the type that plugs into an outlet) be continually used to safeguard against any future CO contamination. Do not be misled by a contractor who gives your home a clean bill of health, even though your CO detector has been activated. The contractor's detection device may be of an inexpensive variety (a good hand-held tester can cost $2000 or more) and may be giving a false reading.

CO in the home is a byproduct of natural gas combustion. It is a poisonous gas that inhibits the blood's ability to carry oxygen throughout the body. CO is insidious in that it is invisible, odorless, tasteless, and can be lethal.

Common Household Sources of CO Are:

♦ Gas-burning fireplace
♦ Gas dryer
♦ Cracked heat exchanger in furnace
♦ Gas kitchen stove
♦ Refrigerator
♦ Grill—in an enclosed area
♦ Water heater
♦ Clogged chimney

Because new homes are more tightly sealed, CO is more of a problem today than it was in decades past. Due to the lack of insulation in the walls, old homes allowed more exchange of air with the outside. Today's homes not only have walls and ceilings packed with insulation, but the walls have plastic wraps applied to them. Add a plastic vapor barrier in the ceiling and it is hard to imagine a more sealed environment.

Recently a curious phenomenon occurred here in Iowa. CO detectors were showing the presence of this gas in homes. But when homeowners had inspections carried out, no source of CO could be detected. There were no cracked heat exchangers in furnaces and all flues were venting properly. Speculation was that the CO detectors were faulty. Contractors were finding no mechanical defects leaving the homeowner to believe that all was well. An Iowa State University engineer in Ames cleverly pointed to "backdrafting" as the source of the CO. Fumes that should be venting up the flue or chimney were being sucked through the house by an exhaust fan. In other words, spent gas fumes that normally rise up the chimney can be drawn by the hood fan over the stove or the exhaust fan in the bath (see Figure 10–1 on the following page). New houses are so air tight that, if an exhaust fan runs for any length of time, it has no place to draw air from other than flues and chimneys. The recommendation, therefore, is to run exhaust fans only for a limited amount of time, particularly during the months

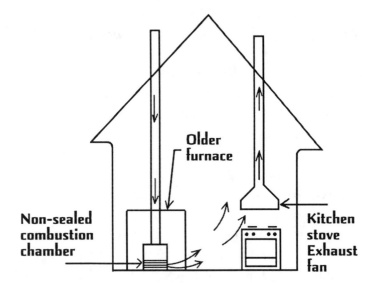

Figure 10–1 Backdrafting

when the furnace is operating.   New combustion furnaces and hot water heater burners are sealed and cannot backdraft or otherwise allow CO into the living quarters of the home (see Figure 10–2 on following page).

Radon

Radon is a radioactive gas produced by the natural breakdown of uranium in the soil. (It is also a by-product of farm fertilizers.) It readily seeps from the ground through cracks (even small ones) in the basement floor or walls. It is a naturally occurring hazard that, like CO, is odorless, tasteless, and invisible.   The U.S. Environmental Protection

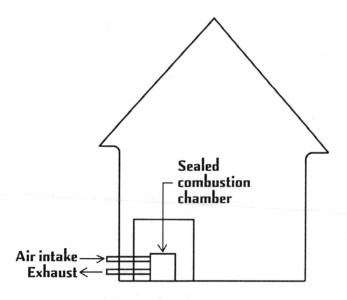

Figure 10-2 New Furnace

Agency (EPA) estimates that radon is the second leading cause of lung cancer in the U.S. Charcoal canisters are recommended by the EPA as a simple, cost-effective way of obtaining quick "screening" measurements of indoor radon. The EPA also warns that, to be considered safe, levels of radon should be below 4.0 Picocuries per liter (pCi/1). The average level of radon in homes is 1.5 pCi/1 and anything over 4.0 pCi/1 should be professionally corrected.

Though there are plenty of companies that deal with this problem, I would not feel comfortable buying a home with excessive radon levels. Reduction techniques include ventilating the soil around the home and sealing any and all cracks in the basement walls and floor. Doubts exist as to the long-term effectiveness of these procedures. Who could live with continually examining the basement for new cracks and checking and replacing caulk, fearing a re-invasion of this menace?

Testing for radon is recommended every two to three years if the reading is acceptable. Considering the risks of radon and the lack of a sure, permanent solution to the problem if levels are too high, I would recommend doing what my wife Deb and I did when we found our ideal home. We reached an agreement with the sellers that they would carry out a radon test at our expense while we waited on the preliminary transactions of the home sale. This simple test requires opening a charcoal canister, placing it in the home for three days, sealing it, and mailing it to the manufacturer for analysis. Radon test kits are available at hardware stores. A seller cannot refuse a radon test without appearing to be hiding something. It should be a condition in your offer to buy the home that radon levels must be below 4.0 pCi/1. We repeated the radon test after taking possession of the home to verify that it had been done objectively.

Chapter 11
The Real Estate Agent

Most homes for sale are listed through a real estate agency and involve dealing with a real estate agent. It is extremely important for you to be aware of the many features and factors involved with this service and with home selection since the main responsibility for protecting your interests lies with you. Many factors can affect the realtor's ability to provide the important information that will enable you to make an informed decision on a home purchase.

Since realtors provide home inspectors with a large part of their business, it can sometimes be difficult to obtain an accurate, objective report on a house. People in the market for a home may ask their realtor to recommend a home inspector. Of course, it is in the realtor's interest that the home inspector not find major faults. I've seen first-hand evidence of inadequate inspections. In this circumstance, a faulty house may be misrepresented to be OK.

Conversely, while I am on the subject, I should mention another problem with inspections. I was reminded of it by a longtime customer who was selling his home. In Iowa, no official licensing board exists for them, so there are no mandatory requirements for doing business as a home inspector. Consequently, there seems to be an abundance of "inspectors" confusing and alarming both buyers and sellers—sometimes needlessly. While respectable, professional home inspectors do exist, some inspectors seem determined to compile a list of defects on any given home, regardless of its quality. Nearly perfect homes may be portrayed as being full of deficiencies. An inspector can drive a car with AAA Inspections on the door, spout a small vocabulary of building terms, and the customer will assume they are legitimate. They are scaring the daylights out of people and stalling sales of homes over ridiculously minor items such as the corners of basically good shingles being elevated ¼" off the roof, which was the case with my friend.

I suspect some of these "inspectors" lack the skills to detect and elaborate on serious defects and instead try to establish credibility by citing numerous minor things less likely to be challenged. So in Iowa, as in many other states, the competency of home inspectors is uncertain. These questionable inspections point up the advantages of equipping yourself with a good fundamental working knowledge of the home.

There is a lot to be said for buying a for-sale-by-owner home. The price is usually much better. You may be sure that a realtor will price the house as high as the market will allow. And remember that the house may be a great buy and still unsold only because it has not been widely advertised. Conversely, houses sold by realtors that are of exceptional quality do not remain on the market long. Unfortunately, for-sale-by-owner homes may be so few that it may be necessary to seek a realtor's help. Still, keep your eyes open for the private sale.

The important thing to remember about the real estate agent is that, though he may be looking for a home for you, he is not working for you. It is not his primary consideration to satisfy your wants and needs. He represents the seller's interest, in exchange for six or seven percent of the sale price which he customarily divides with the broker he is working for. I recently asked a long-time realtor in Iowa City how much information on defects he relates to the buyer. His response was, "Only the things we might get sued for." Remember this: If you are the buyer, the realtor is working for the seller. If you are the seller, he is working for himself. So do not be overly influenced by the realtor's efforts to make you buy. It is true that it does not pay to delay, especially if the property you are inspecting has just come on the market and it appears to be exactly what you are looking for. On the other hand, you need to take sufficient time to consider all the relevant information about the house. The realtor, in his capacity as a salesman, will have many methods for stampeding you into making a decision. A classic example is that of telling you that he has another party interested in your dream house! Do not be rushed. The chances are that, if there is another party and if that other party is sensible, he too will be unlikely to make an uninformed, hasty decision on the home.

Remember, perseverance and discrimination are absolutely vital to home buying. You should not concern yourself about causing the real estate agent stress. You should also be prepared to politely ignore his/her friendly chatter as it may distract you from the business of inspection. Remember that the real estate agent generally has little knowledge about the mechanics of a home. His comments are more or less meaningless generalities about the house being "extremely well built," etc.

I had three different real estate companies looking for me before I bought my current home. I had them all at their wit's end. (Ultimately I bought a for-sale-by-owner home.) I would have an agent show me ten houses in a single day. About thirty percent of these homes I ruled out from the curb. I know that these agents would like to have caused me bodily harm despite their smiles and polite conversation! Deb and I had the perfect game plan for our inspections. She would size up the home for room size, closet space, washer/dryer hook-ups and things of that nature, while I inspected it for structural and other defects. All the while the real estate agent would be trying to keep up with us, thoroughly confused by our organization and obviously flustered at his loss of control of the situation. Politely ignore the realtor and focus on the inspection.

Rules governing realty transactions may exist in your state as provided by a real estate commission or licensing board. These rules will take into account state laws governing real estate matters. Copies should be available to you through your state Department of Commerce or your Secretary of State's office. You should get a copy and review it to insure that your rights are protected. In Iowa, a state law enacted in 1993 (effective July 1, 1994) mandates that a disclosure of certain known conditions of the home be made available to the buyer. Prior to its existence, the sale of a home was pretty much "as is" or "buyer beware." Mandatory disclosures are becoming the law in more and more states. From the buyer's perspective this is obviously all to the good. It would certainly improve the prospects of a lawsuit were it to be established that a problem existed; that there had been repeated servicing by, say, Jones Roofing; and that the condition of the roof (as having had no leaks) had nevertheless been misrepresented.

Another piece of important information on disclosure statements was given to me by a friend who is a Realtor. His experience has taught him to be skeptical of a disclosure statement that lists absolutely no deficiencies in a particular home. A total lack of deficiencies may be true in a home less than five years old or in an extremely high-quality home that is immaculately maintained. However, 99% of homes on the market fall into neither category. So, my advice would be to inspect especially carefully in a home with a disclosure statement that Realtors describe as "too clean."

Summary

In view of the fact that home buying/relocating causes stress second only to losing a loved one, prepare for it as if going into battle. Keep a lookout for for-sale-by-owner homes and supplement this by using one or more real estate agents. Be patient. By the time I found my home, I had both the real estate agents AND Deb mad. But now we have one of the best homes in town, solid as a rock.

If disclosure is law in your state, a copy should be readily available from either the owner (for-sale-by-owner) or the real estate agent if the property is listed. Look it over carefully as you inspect. If disclosure is not law, the response to a request for one might be revealing.

Figure 11–1 on the following page is a sample disclosure statement. Figure 11–2 on pages 122–125 provides a copy of the disclosure statement required by Iowa law. Your state most likely has a similar disclosure statement.

Figure 11–1

RESIDENTIAL PROPERTY SELLER DISCLOSURE STATEMENT

RESIDENTIAL PROPERTY SELLER DISCLOSURE STATEMENT

Property Address: _____

PURPOSE:

Use this statement to disclose information as required by Iowa Code Supplement chapter 558A. This law requires certain sellers of residential property that includes at least one and no more than four dwelling units, to disclose information about the property to be sold. The following disclosures are made by the seller(s) and not by any agent acting on behalf of the seller(s).

INSTRUCTIONS TO SELLER(S).

1. Seller(s) must complete this statement. Respond to all questions, or attach reports allowed by Iowa Code Supplement section 558A.4(2);
2. Disclose all known conditions materially affecting this property;
3. If an item does not apply to this property, indicate it is not applicable (N/A);
4. Please provide information in good faith and make a reasonable effort to ascertain the required information. If the required information is unknown or is unavailable following a reasonable effort, use an approximation of the information, or indicate that the information is unknown (UNK). All approximations must be identified as approximations (AP).
5. Additional pages may be attached as needed;
6. Keep a copy of this statement with your other important papers.

		Yes	No
1.	Basement/Foundation: Any known water or other problems?	☐	☐
2.	Roof: Any known problems?	☐	☐
	Any known repairs?	☐	☐
	If yes, date of repair/replacement: ___/___/___		

...nd Pump: Any known prob... ...tion with adjo... ...ch as walls, | Yes ☐ No ☐
...repairs? ...sponsibility may h... | Yes ☐ No ☐
ro... ...ways whose use or m... an effect on the property? ___/___/___

Any known "common areas" such as pools, tennis courts, walkways, or other areas co-owned with others, or a Homeowner's Association which has any authority over the property? Yes ☐ No ☐

17. Physical Problems: Any known settling, flooding, drainage or grading problems? Yes ☐ No ☐

18. Structural Damage: Any known structural damage? Yes ☐ No ☐

You **MUST** explain any "YES" response(s) above. Use the back of this statement or additional sheets as necessary:

_____
_____
_____

SELLER(S) DISCLOSURE:

Seller(s) discloses the information regarding this property based on information known or reasonably available to the Seller(s). The Seller(s) has owned the property since ___/___ The Seller(s) certifies that as of the date signed this information is true and accurate to the best of my/our knowledge.

Seller _____   Seller _____

Date ___/___/___   Date ___/___/___

BUYER(S) ACKNOWLEDGMENT:

Buyer(s) acknowledges receipt of a copy of this Real Estate Disclosure Statement. This statement is not intended to be a warranty or to substitute for any inspection the buyer(s) may wish to obtain.

Buyer _____   Buyer _____

Date ___/___/___   Date ___/___/___

Figure 11-2

RESIDENTIAL PROPERTY SELLER DISCLOSURE STATEMENT

Property Address: _____

PURPOSE:

Use this statement to disclose information as required by Iowa Code Supplement chapter 558A. This law requires certain sellers of residential property that includes at least one and no more than four dwelling units, to disclose information about the property to be sold. The following disclosures are made by the seller(s) and not by any agent acting on behalf of the seller(s).

INSTRUCTIONS TO SELLER(S).

1. Seller(s) must complete this statement. Respond to all questions, or attach reports allowed by Iowa Code Supplement section 558A.4(2);
2. Disclose all known conditions materially affecting this property;
3. If an item does not apply to this property, indicate it is not applicable (N/A);
4. Please provide information in good faith and make a responsible effort to ascertain the required information. If the required information is unknown or is unavailable following a reasonable effort, use an approximation of the information, or indicate that the information is unknown (UNK). All approximations must be identified as approximations (AP).
5. Additional pages may be attached as needed;
6. Keep a copy of this statement with your other important papers.

Figure 11–2
RESIDENTIAL PROPERTY SELLER
DISCLOSURE STATEMENT (continued)

1. Basement/Foundation: Any known water or other problems? Yes ☐ No ☐

2. Roof: Any known problems? Yes ☐ No ☐
   Any known repairs? Yes ☐ No ☐
   If yes, date of repair/replacement: ___/___/____

3. Well and Pump: Any known problems? Yes ☐ No ☐
   Any known repairs? Yes ☐ No ☐
   If yes, date of repairs/replacement: ___/___/____
   Any known water tests? Yes ☐ No ☐
   If yes, date of last report: ___/___/____
   and results: _____

4. Septic Tanks/Drain Fields: Any known problems? Yes ☐ No ☐
   Location of Tank: _____
   Date tank last cleaned: ___/___/____

5. Sewer System: Any known problems? Yes ☐ No ☐
   Any known repairs? Yes ☐ No ☐
   If Yes, date of repairs/replacement: ___/___/____

6. Heating System(s):
   Any known problems? Yes ☐ No ☐
   Any known repairs? Yes ☐ No ☐
   If yes, date of repairs/replacement: ___/___/____

7. Central Cooling System(s):
   Any known problems? Yes ☐ No ☐
   Any known repairs? Yes ☐ No ☐
   If yes, date of repairs/replacement: ___/___/____

Figure 11–2
RESIDENTIAL PROPERTY SELLER
DISCLOSURE STATEMENT (continued)

8. Plumbing System(s):
    Any known problems?   Yes ☐ No ☐
    Any known repairs?   Yes ☐ No ☐
    If yes, date of repairs/replacement: ___/___/____

9. Electrical System(s):
    Any known problems?   Yes ☐ No ☐
    Any known repairs?   Yes ☐ No ☐
    If yes, date of repairs/replacement: ___/___/____

10. Pest Infestation: (e.g. termites, carpenter ants)
    Any known problems?   Yes ☐ No ☐
    If yes, date(s) of treatment: ___/___/____
    Any known structural damage?   Yes ☐ No ☐
    If yes, date of repairs/replacement: ___/___/____

11. Asbestos:
    Any known to be present in the structure? Yes ☐ No ☐
    If yes, explain: _____

12. Radon: Any known tests for the presence
    of radon gas?   Yes ☐ No ☐
    If yes, date of last report: ___/___/____
    And results: _____

13. Lead Based Paint: Any known to be present in the
    structure?   Yes ☐ No ☐

14. Flood Plain: Do you know if the property is located in a
    flood plain?   Yes ☐ No ☐
    If yes, what is the flood plan designation: _____

15. Zoning: Do you know the zoning classification of the
    property?   Yes ☐ No ☐
    If yes, what is the zoning classification: _____

Figure 11-2
RESIDENTIAL PROPERTY SELLER
DISCLOSURE STATEMENT (continued)

16. Shared or Co-Owned Features: Any features of the property known to be shared in common with adjoining landowners, such as walls, fences, roads, and driveways whose use or maintenance responsibility may have an effect on the property? Yes ☐ No ☐

    Any known "common areas" such as pools, tennis courts, walkways, or other areas co-owned with others, or a Homeowner's Association which has any authority over the property? Yes ☐ No ☐

17. Physical Problems: Any known settling, flooding, drainage, or grading problems? Yes ☐ No ☐

18. Structural Damage: Any known structural damage? Yes ☐ No ☐

You **MUST** explain any "Yes" response(s) above. Use the back of this statement or additional sheets as necessary:

_____

_____

Figure 11–2
RESIDENTIAL PROPERTY SELLER
DISCLOSURE STATEMENT (continued)

SELLER(S) DISCLOSURE:

Seller(s) discloses the information regarding this property based on information known or reasonably available to the Seller(s). The Seller(s) has owned the property since ___/___/____. The Seller(s) certifies that as of the date signed this information is true and accurate to the best of my/our knowledge.

Seller _____ Seller _____

Date _____/_____/_____ Date _____/_____/_____

BUYER(S) ACKNOWLEDGEMENT:

Buyer(s) acknowledges receipt of a copy of this Real Estate Disclosure Statement. This statement is not intended to be a warranty or to substitute for any inspection the buyer(s) may wish to obtain.

Buyer _____ Buyer _____

Date _____/_____/_____ Date _____/_____/_____

Chapter 12
General Advice

Gutters

Replacement of gutters on the average home will run several hundred dollars, which is significant enough to warrant at least a quick look at the ones on our prospective home. Look for stains or rust along the bottom edge of the gutters, which indicates leakage. If you happen to be looking at the home during a winter month, there may be snow sitting in the gutter and subsequent leaking from problem gutter joints may show as you are making your inspection.

As a rule, leaking gutters will need to be replaced. Most repairs on leaky joints don't hold and rust is usually associated with the problem. On the other hand, if you have aluminum gutters that are properly sloped to the downspouts, repair rather than replacement would generally be advisable. If you have an opportunity to look inside the gutters, do so. Many gutters on homes twenty-five years old and older are made of steel. Typically they are painted and can look great from the ground, but may be heavily rusted on the inside. Again, the possible need for gutter replacement is no cause for panic—it is just information you should have.

My gutters are badly rusted. I'll replace them soon with the standard K-style gutter and I'll use the newer aluminum seamless gutters. The gutter contractor shapes the gutter right on the job site out of a flat roll of aluminum. The only seams are at the corners of your house.

Gutters are no longer restricted to a white or galvanized finish. New gutters come in a wide range of baked-on enameled finishes. I would recommend paying a little more and getting heavier gauge aluminum. It holds up well to ladders set against it. Standard gutter thickness is .027 inch, but thicker .032 inch gutters are available and are the better choice.

Soffit Rot

If you are buying an older, one-and-a-half or two-story home, it is not uncommon to see decorative boards used for the underside of the soffit. They are usually 3¼" wide with a bead down the center. They are joined in a tongue and groove fashion and are referred to as bead-board or beaded ceiling. It is not unusual to discover that these soffits have some rot or otherwise need work. I mention this because bead boards sized to match the old ones are hard to find. If a cabinet maker has to grind a new knife to shape these boards for you, the cost will be considerable. Also, work on overhangs or soffits is itself a pricey proposition since the area is so hard to reach from a ladder. Proper repairs on a soffit may require the construction of scaffolding. Though I would not reject a good home just because of the need for soffit repairs, it is important to know that a considerable amount of work will be necessary.

Grade Work

Grade work is particularly important around a home and often is inadequate. The grade should slope away from the foundation (see Figure 12–1 below). Grade work that slopes away from the house

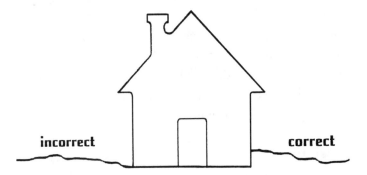

Figure 12–1 Foundation Gradework

quickly carries water away. Grade work sloping towards the house channels water down alongside either the foundation or the basement wall with unfortunate results. Not only does this water reduce the prospects of having a dry basement, but (as indicated before) it freezes, thaws, and refreezes in the winter months creating a hydraulic press effect on the walls that produces movement and cracking. Remember that these foundation walls support the entire house. The slope away from the foundation should drop at least 6" in 10'.

Windows

Window inspection should be a part of your overall inspection of a home. It should not be taken for granted that all windows are good, and remember that window replacement is expensive. For instance, a good, average-size replacement window, 34" wide x 46" high, would cost around $300, not including installation. If the house has unusual siding (such as brick) which is hard to modify to accept standard-sized windows, the price would be even higher since the replacement windows would have to be custom made to fit the old opening. You might pay $500 or more per window.

Wintertime is ideal for checking windows. If either the primary window or the storm window leaks air, there will be telltale condensation or frost on the pane. The rule for determining which window is leaking is as follows: (a) if condensation is on the interior side of the primary window, the storm window is leaking air and (b) if condensation is on the interior side of the storm window, it is the primary window that is leaking air. The condensation indicates where the cold air is meeting the warm air.

If the storm windows leak badly (lots of condensation on the primary windowpane), water accumulation will soak the wooden sash of the primary window and eventually ruin it. If the primary window leaks badly, water will accumulate between the primary and storm windows, soaking and ruining the windowsill. It is very important to look for condensation on the windows if you are home shopping in the winter.

Regardless of the season, it is important to inspect the windows from the exterior. I wouldn't panic if I saw a little rot on either the side or top casings (brickmold) around the window. However, if the sill (board at the bottom) of the window shows rot, that's a different matter. You would be hard pressed to find a carpenter who hasn't been on a repair call to a house with rotted windowsills. Homeowners see this rot and assume the board can be easily removed and replaced. It is rather difficult to explain that the sill is integrally joined to the side jambs (see Figure 12-2 on the following page) and that, to make the repair, the window has to be removed. It is a major undertaking for such a small area of rot. Customers are invariably shocked at the cost.

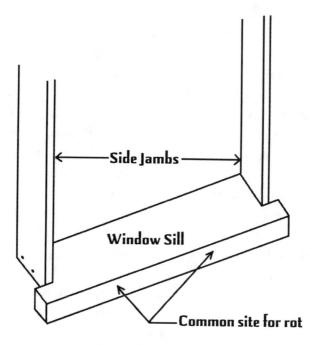

Figure 12-2 Window Construction

Location

Remember the old adage? The three most important considerations in real estate are location, location, and location. I would agree. The ultimate in urban home location would be prestigious older neighborhoods formed long ago by prominent citizens seeking the best location for view, proximity to places of interest, and with little thorough-fare traffic. Interestingly, some of these old neighborhoods were started when a distinguished individual (such as Mr. Manville of Manville Heights here in Iowa City) chose a particular hill to build on and his friends and colleagues followed suit. Typically, homes in these fashionable neighborhoods are of high quality and durable, the craftsmanship being excellent, so that high property values are permanent. If you are in the appropriate income bracket, you need hardly look further.

If, on the other hand, a middle-class neighborhood is more suited to your income, the following advice may be helpful. A long time ago, a friend told me how to size up a neighborhood. Simply drive there and park for an hour or two at different times of the day, on several different days. This is an excellent way of getting a feel for the area you are considering.

If at all possible, introduce yourself to a neighbor of your prospective house. Ask questions such as:

1. Have real estate taxes been increasing during the past few years?
2. Are home values increasing or decreasing in the neighborhood?
3. Does there seem to be a trend of exodus from the neighborhood?
4. Is neighborhood crime at a minimum?

Also, make your own observations as to the following:

♦ Is the neighborhood polluted with noise or heavy traffic?

♦ Are there signs of litter?

♦ Are surrounding homes and yards unkempt?

♦ Are there suspiciously vacant homes in the neighborhood?

♦ Are there any factories to the west of the home? (A prevailing west wind might bring poor quality air.)

♦ Are the cars in the neighborhood old? Are there any derelict cars around?

Chapter 13
Summary/Checklist

Bear in mind that the aim of this book is not to provide a comprehensive, detailed analysis of all mechanical aspects of the home. I did not mention broken windowpanes, worn carpet, or cracks in the bathroom sink because I considered such items as relatively minor. Instead, it focuses on common problems or defects that may seriously depreciate a property. It is a manual to help guide you safely through the ordeal of buying a home.

I believe that this book will help you in several ways. If you opt not to have a home professionally inspected, it is of obvious value in helping you personally determine advantages or possible problems. If you do want to have a prospective home professionally evaluated and it is practical to do so, you can minimize the number of inspections by first conducting your own screenings. This book will also make you better able to judge the competency of a professional home inspector. Even if you are not presently in the market to buy a home, the information contained here will be useful to you as a householder.

In the following lists, I have grouped together all the key checkpoints given in the book. An asterisk indicates items that may be a critical defect. One or more critical defects would warrant careful further inspection. I would suggest providing yourself with as many copies of this checklist as you anticipate you will need. Extra copies of the checklists are provided at end of this book. You may remove or photocopy them to use. A clipboard would be handy as a solid writing surface. At the top of the page, identify the house by its address and also by some physical characteristic such as "yellow house on corner lot."

The checklist is in an order that will allow you to make your inspection in one tour without retracing your steps. If you try to inspect each system individually (chapter by chapter), for electrical you would go downstairs to view the service panel, upstairs to see the outlets, and outside to look at the service drop. To inspect the plumbing, go downstairs again to inspect the pipes, back upstairs to check the bath fixtures, etc. ... I think you see the problem.

Incidentally, save the checklist for the home you ultimately buy. It might be nice to include in your family album for sentimental reflection in the future. I believe that, after a few rehearsals in your present home and a couple of tours of the real thing, you will find yourself quite comfortable with this procedure which will become routine. I shall refrain from saying "good luck" as I am confident that at this point you are well beyond reliance on luck and instead are well armed with knowledge. I wish you well.

Greg

Exterior Checklist

(May remove or copy this page to use.)

House: _____ Details: _____

_____ 1960 or earlier vintage (or evidence of exceptional quality)

_____ Tri-plex service drop

_____ Shade trees

_____ Clapboard, vinyl, brick (no movement, good mortar), or good aluminum siding. Prefer no masonite or T-111. No rough-sawn clapboard unless willing to let it weather.

_____ Exposed foundation looks good (good mortar too)*

_____ Grade slopes away from house

_____ House appears plumb and level*

_____ Minimal skylights or flat areas on roof*

_____ No excessive shingle build-up

_____ Shingles appear good

_____ Straight lines as you sight across roof—no bulges or depressions*

_____ No evidence of insect infestation

_____ Soffit rot

_____ Gutters leaking, in disrepair

_____ Windows O.K.—no sill rot*

_____ Good location/neighborhood

*May indicate a critical defect. One or more critical defects would warrant careful further inspection.

Interior Checklist

(May remove or copy this page to use.)

House: _____ Details: _____

_____   Grounded outlets*

_____   Drains and stool empty quickly *

_____   Good water pressure*

_____   Walls and floors reasonably plumb and level*

_____   Doors close well—no large cracks in plaster at tops of door casings*

_____   No signs of roof leakage

_____   Acceptable results of radon test (if home is a finalist)*

_____   Window condensation minimal (if checked in winter)*

*May indicate a critical defect. One or more critical defects would warrant careful further inspection.

Basement Checklist
(May remove or copy this page to use.)

House: _____   Details: _____

_____   Breaker type electrical service panel—100 amp or greater*

_____   Water softener

_____   Copper or non-corroded galvanized water supply lines*

_____   Furnace and central air units that look and sound good—Brand names?

_____   Basement dry*

_____   Sump pit

_____   Straight walls—mortar intact—no cracks, bulges, mold, or moisture*

_____   Floor drains

_____   1st floor framing appearance*

_____   Check for insect infestation

_____   Washer/dryer hook-ups

Also, remember to obtain and review a disclosure statement, if available, as well as a copy of recent utility bills.

*May indicate a critical defect. One or more critical defects would warrant careful further inspection.

Index

How To Order
A Carpenter's Advice on Buying a Home

Single copies may be ordered directly from publisher:

Canary Connect Publications
A Division of SOBOLE, Inc.
PO Box 5317
Coralville, IA 52241–0317

www.canaryconnect.com

Phone: (319) 351–2317
FAX: (319) 354–8001
Toll Free: (877) 536–5344

With your order, enclose payment of $14.95 + $2.50
(shipping/handling) for a total of $17.45.
Iowa residents also add $.75 sales tax.
MasterCard and VISA accepted.
US Funds only.

Quantity discounts are also available.

Other Books from Canary Connect Publications

Allergy & *Candida* Cooking Made Easy
by Sondra K. Lewis
with Lonnett Dietrich Blakley

For pricing and ordering information,
use contact information above.

About the Author

Greg Evans is a builder from the Midwest whose trade includes all aspects of home building and remodeling. He has a total of 22 years of home-building experience with expertise in the areas of cabinetry, carpentry, electrical wiring, and plumbing. Greg lives in Iowa City, Iowa, with his wife Deb, daughters Sidney and Abby, and son Joseph.

Exterior Checklist
(May remove or copy this page to use.)

House: _____ Details: _____

_____ 1960 or earlier vintage (or evidence of exceptional quality)

_____ Tri-plex service drop

_____ Shade trees

_____ Clapboard, vinyl, brick (no movement, good mortar), or good aluminum siding. Prefer no masonite or T-111. No rough-sawn clapboard unless willing to let it weather.

_____ Exposed foundation looks good (good mortar too)*

_____ Grade slopes away from house

_____ House appears plumb and level*

_____ Minimal skylights or flat areas on roof*

_____ No excessive shingle build-up

_____ Shingles appear good

_____ Straight lines as you sight across roof—no bulges or depressions*

_____ No evidence of insect infestation

_____ Soffit rot

_____ Gutters leaking, in disrepair

_____ Windows O.K.—no sill rot*

_____ Good location/neighborhood

*May indicate a critical defect. One or more critical defects would warrant careful further inspection.

Interior Checklist

(May remove or copy this page to use.)

House: _____ Details: _____

_____   Grounded outlets*

_____   Drains and stool empty quickly *

_____   Good water pressure*

_____   Walls and floors reasonably plumb and level*

_____   Doors close well—no large cracks in plaster at tops of door casings*

_____   No signs of roof leakage

_____   Acceptable results of radon test (if home is a finalist)*

_____   Window condensation minimal (if checked in winter)*

*May indicate a critical defect. One or more critical defects would warrant careful further inspection.

Basement Checklist
(May remove or copy this page to use.)

House: _____ Details: _____

_____ Breaker type electrical service panel—100 amp or greater*

_____ Water softener

_____ Copper or non-corroded galvanized water supply lines*

_____ Furnace and central air units that look and sound good—Brand names?

_____ Basement dry*

_____ Sump pit

_____ Straight walls—mortar intact—no cracks, bulges, mold, or moisture*

_____ Floor drains

_____ 1st floor framing appearance*

_____ Check for insect infestation

_____ Washer/dryer hook-ups

Also, remember to obtain and review a disclosure statement, if available, as well as a copy of recent utility bills.

*May indicate a critical defect. One or more critical defects would warrant careful further inspection.

Exterior Checklist

(May remove or copy this page to use.)

House: _____ Details: _____

_____ 1960 or earlier vintage (or evidence of exceptional quality)

_____ Tri-plex service drop

_____ Shade trees

_____ Clapboard, vinyl, brick (no movement, good mortar), or good aluminum siding. Prefer no masonite or T-111. No rough-sawn clapboard unless willing to let it weather.

_____ Exposed foundation looks good (good mortar too)*

_____ Grade slopes away from house

_____ House appears plumb and level*

_____ Minimal skylights or flat areas on roof*

_____ No excessive shingle build-up

_____ Shingles appear good

_____ Straight lines as you sight across roof—no bulges or depressions*

_____ No evidence of insect infestation

_____ Soffit rot

_____ Gutters leaking, in disrepair

_____ Windows O.K.—no sill rot*

_____ Good location/neighborhood

*May indicate a critical defect. One or more critical defects would warrant careful further inspection.

Interior Checklist

(May remove or copy this page to use.)

House: _____ Details: _____

_____ Grounded outlets*

_____ Drains and stool empty quickly *

_____ Good water pressure*

_____ Walls and floors reasonably plumb and level*

_____ Doors close well—no large cracks in plaster at tops of door casings*

_____ No signs of roof leakage

_____ Acceptable results of radon test (if home is a finalist)*

_____ Window condensation minimal (if checked in winter)*

*May indicate a critical defect. One or more critical defects would warrant careful further inspection.

Basement Checklist
(May remove or copy this page to use.)

House: _____ Details: _____

_____ Breaker type electrical service panel— 100 amp or greater*

_____ Water softener

_____ Copper or non-corroded galvanized water supply lines*

_____ Furnace and central air units that look and sound good—Brand names?

_____ Basement dry*

_____ Sump pit

_____ Straight walls—mortar intact—no cracks, bulges, mold, or moisture*

_____ Floor drains

_____ 1st floor framing appearance*

_____ Check for insect infestation

_____ Washer/dryer hook-ups

Also, remember to obtain and review a disclosure statement, if available, as well as a copy of recent utility bills.

*May indicate a critical defect. One or more critical defects would warrant careful further inspection.

Exterior Checklist

(May remove or copy this page to use.)

House: _____ Details: _____

_____ 1960 or earlier vintage (or evidence of exceptional quality)

_____ Tri-plex service drop

_____ Shade trees

_____ Clapboard, vinyl, brick (no movement, good mortar), or good aluminum siding. Prefer no masonite or T-111. No rough-sawn clapboard unless willing to let it weather.

_____ Exposed foundation looks good (good mortar too)*

_____ Grade slopes away from house

_____ House appears plumb and level*

_____ Minimal skylights or flat areas on roof*

_____ No excessive shingle build-up

_____ Shingles appear good

_____ Straight lines as you sight across roof—no bulges or depressions*

_____ No evidence of insect infestation

_____ Soffit rot

_____ Gutters leaking, in disrepair

_____ Windows O.K.—no sill rot*

_____ Good location/neighborhood

*May indicate a critical defect. One or more critical defects would warrant careful further inspection.

Interior Checklist

(May remove or copy this page to use.)

House: _____ Details: _____

_____ Grounded outlets*

_____ Drains and stool empty quickly *

_____ Good water pressure*

_____ Walls and floors reasonably plumb and level*

_____ Doors close well—no large cracks in plaster at tops of door casings*

_____ No signs of roof leakage

_____ Acceptable results of radon test (if home is a finalist)*

_____ Window condensation minimal (if checked in winter)*

*May indicate a critical defect. One or more critical defects would warrant careful further inspection.

Basement Checklist
(May remove or copy this page to use.)

House: _____ Details: _____

_____ Breaker type electrical service panel— 100 amp or greater*

_____ Water softener

_____ Copper or non-corroded galvanized water supply lines*

_____ Furnace and central air units that look and sound good—Brand names?

_____ Basement dry*

_____ Sump pit

_____ Straight walls—mortar intact—no cracks, bulges, mold, or moisture*

_____ Floor drains

_____ 1st floor framing appearance*

_____ Check for insect infestation

_____ Washer/dryer hook-ups

Also, remember to obtain and review a disclosure statement, if available, as well as a copy of recent utility bills.

*May indicate a critical defect. One or more critical defects would warrant careful further inspection.

Exterior Checklist

(May remove or copy this page to use.)

House: _____ Details: _____

_____ 1960 or earlier vintage (or evidence of exceptional quality)

_____ Tri-plex service drop

_____ Shade trees

_____ Clapboard, vinyl, brick (no movement, good mortar), or good aluminum siding. Prefer no masonite or T-111. No rough-sawn clapboard unless willing to let it weather.

_____ Exposed foundation looks good (good mortar too)*

_____ Grade slopes away from house

_____ House appears plumb and level*

_____ Minimal skylights or flat areas on roof*

_____ No excessive shingle build-up

_____ Shingles appear good

_____ Straight lines as you sight across roof—no bulges or depressions*

_____ No evidence of insect infestation

_____ Soffit rot

_____ Gutters leaking, in disrepair

_____ Windows O.K.—no sill rot*

_____ Good location/neighborhood

*May indicate a critical defect. One or more critical defects would warrant careful further inspection.

Interior Checklist

(May remove or copy this page to use.)

House: _____ Details: _____

_____ Grounded outlets*

_____ Drains and stool empty quickly *

_____ Good water pressure*

_____ Walls and floors reasonably plumb and level*

_____ Doors close well—no large cracks in plaster at tops of door casings*

_____ No signs of roof leakage

_____ Acceptable results of radon test (if home is a finalist)*

_____ Window condensation minimal (if checked in winter)*

*May indicate a critical defect. One or more critical defects would warrant careful further inspection.

Basement Checklist

(May remove or copy this page to use.)

House: _____ Details: _____

_____ Breaker type electrical service panel— 100 amp or greater*

_____ Water softener

_____ Copper or non-corroded galvanized water supply lines*

_____ Furnace and central air units that look and sound good—Brand names?

_____ Basement dry*

_____ Sump pit

_____ Straight walls—mortar intact—no cracks, bulges, mold, or moisture*

_____ Floor drains

_____ 1st floor framing appearance*

_____ Check for insect infestation

_____ Washer/dryer hook-ups

Also, remember to obtain and review a disclosure statement, if available, as well as a copy of recent utility bills.

*May indicate a critical defect. One or more critical defects would warrant careful further inspection.

Exterior Checklist
(May remove or copy this page to use.)

House: _____ Details: _____

_____ 1960 or earlier vintage (or evidence of exceptional quality)

_____ Tri-plex service drop

_____ Shade trees

_____ Clapboard, vinyl, brick (no movement, good mortar), or good aluminum siding. Prefer no masonite or T-111. No rough-sawn clapboard unless willing to let it weather.

_____ Exposed foundation looks good (good mortar too)*

_____ Grade slopes away from house

_____ House appears plumb and level*

_____ Minimal skylights or flat areas on roof*

_____ No excessive shingle build-up

_____ Shingles appear good

_____ Straight lines as you sight across roof—no bulges or depressions*

_____ No evidence of insect infestation

_____ Soffit rot

_____ Gutters leaking, in disrepair

_____ Windows O.K.—no sill rot*

_____ Good location/neighborhood

*May indicate a critical defect. One or more critical defects would warrant careful further inspection.

Interior Checklist
(May remove or copy this page to use.)

House: _____ Details: _____

_____   Grounded outlets*

_____   Drains and stool empty quickly *

_____   Good water pressure*

_____   Walls and floors reasonably plumb and level*

_____   Doors close well—no large cracks in plaster at tops of door casings*

_____   No signs of roof leakage

_____   Acceptable results of radon test (if home is a finalist)*

_____   Window condensation minimal (if checked in winter)*

*May indicate a critical defect. One or more critical defects would warrant careful further inspection.

Basement Checklist
(May remove or copy this page to use.)

House: _____ Details: _____

_____ Breaker type electrical service panel—100 amp or greater*

_____ Water softener

_____ Copper or non-corroded galvanized water supply lines*

_____ Furnace and central air units that look and sound good—Brand names?

_____ Basement dry*

_____ Sump pit

_____ Straight walls—mortar intact—no cracks, bulges, mold, or moisture*

_____ Floor drains

_____ 1st floor framing appearance*

_____ Check for insect infestation

_____ Washer/dryer hook-ups

Also, remember to obtain and review a disclosure statement, if available, as well as a copy of recent utility bills.

*May indicate a critical defect. One or more critical defects would warrant careful further inspection.